A TEXTBOOK ON DATABASES IN DIGITAL HUMANITIES

A GUIDE TO NON-ENGINEERING BACKGROUND LEARNERS OF LITERARY AND SOCIAL DATA CRITICISM

VALIUR RAHAMAN

Abba Amma

Contents

Foreword

Every discouragement inspires a man to stand against the discouragement and its related factors. I think this is the first book on interdisciplinary studies in humanities and computational database in India. I remember *Introducing Digital Humanities* (2016) of the same author, which was released at one of the premier institutes of India, IIT Indore (in GIAN FDP/ Short Term Course) in the same year, because, it was a unique initiative of a teacher to higher education in India during disciplinary holoquast of humanities and social sciences. This is another initiative that establishes him as a contributor to digital initiatives to humanities teaching and research. The book promotes the new education policy driven higher education in India.

The book rests on a major argument that is integration of databases into humanities education. How it helps a transformative and essential shift in higher education and research. As digital technologies reshape how we access, analyze, and interpret information, integrating databases into humanities teaching becomes a crucial endeavor for advancing scholarship and learning. The integration of databases in humanities education offers opportunities for innovation and engagement. Digital databases provide unprecedented access to a vast array of primary and secondary sources, including rare manuscripts, historical records, and scholarly articles. This democratization of information allows students and researchers to engage with materials that were previously difficult to access, fostering a more inclusive and comprehensive approach to research. Advanced analytical tools, such as text mining, data visualization, and network analysis, enable scholars to uncover patterns, connections, and insights that might not be evident through traditional methods. Databases facilitate interdisciplinary collaboration by bridging the gap between the humanities and other fields, leading to innovative research outcomes and enriching the study of cultural and historical phenomena.

Teaching databases in the humanities opens doors to interactive and experiential learning opportunities, allowing students to create their own projects, conduct analyses, and develop critical thinking skills. This hands-on experience deepens their understanding of the subject matter and prepares them for a digital world. However, there are several challenges that must be addressed: skill development, the digital divide, and preservation and sustainability. Effective use of databases requires specific technical skills, and addressing these issues is essential for maximizing the potential of digital resources.

Looking ahead, the future of database teaching in the humanities promises exciting opportunities for innovation and discovery. By embracing digital technologies and integrating them thoughtfully into humanities education, we can cultivate a new generation of scholars who are well-equipped to navigate and contribute to a digital age.

As we look to the future, the role of databases in the digital humanities will continue to evolve. Emerging technologies, new research methodologies, and expanding datasets will shape the ways in which we use databases to explore humanistic questions. We hope this textbook will serve as a valuable resource for those embarking on this journey and will inspire innovative approaches to digital humanities research and education. I remember words of eminent professor of English, Vikramaditya Rai, my teacher and mentor, that disciplinary networks and connectivity are the outcomes of critical practices. This book is an apt example of his words.

Professor Aziz Haider, President, Shia PG College Lucknow
Former Dean, Humanities, MG Kashi University Varanasi
Lucknow, 2024

Preface

The digital humanities has become a dynamic field that uses databases to explore, interpret, and disseminate humanistic knowledge. This textbook serves as an introduction and detailed resource for those seeking to understand the role of databases in digital humanities. It provides a thorough examination of fundamental concepts, practical techniques, and real-world applications, equipping readers with the knowledge and skills necessary to effectively utilize databases in their research and teaching.

The content is structured to address the needs of a diverse audience, including students new to digital humanities, researchers who wish to incorporate database methodologies into their scholarly work, and educators who aim to integrate database concepts into their curriculum and enhance their teaching with digital tools.

The textbook is organized into several key sections: Foundations of Databases, Database Design and Implementation, Data Analysis and Visualization, Digital Creative Criticism, Literary Database Creation Techniques, and Tools, Projects and other Opportunities, Applications in Digital Humanities, and Ethical and Practical Considerations. The foundations of databases explore fundamental database concepts, such as data models, relational databases, and database management systems (DBMS). Database design and implementation cover data modeling, schema design, and practical aspects of database development and maintenance. Data analysis and visualization explore various techniques for analyzing and visualizing data using databases, such as query languages, data mining, and interactive visualizations.

Lastly, the book emphasizes the responsible use of database technologies in research and education, addressing important issues related to data privacy, ethical considerations, and the long-term sustainability of digital resources. It replies in affirmative to a question: Can we teach database skills to humanities learners?

Valiur Rahaman, Uttar Pradesh

August 2024

Acknowledgements

First of all, I owe with all my senses and organs to Almighty One!

I would like to thank my wife for her understanding, and my children Darshis and Arshis for not complaining too loudly at Dad spending so long in writing.

The creation of this textbook has been an indirect collaborative effort involving experts from various disciplines within the digital humanities. I extend our gratitude to Professor Aziz Haider the mentor, the scholars, critics, practitioners, and educators who contributed their insights and expertise. Their contributions have enriched the content and ensured that it reflects the current state of the field. I am thankful to Lovely Professional University for accepting the initiated proposal on introducing Digital Humanities as a course and program (both UG and PG) in the School of Humanities.

Once more I express innate gratitude to Blessings of Almighty One!

Prologue

The humanities are undergoing a significant transformation due to digital trans-developmental issues. Databases have become a significant innovation in this process, providing structured, searchable, and analyzable repositories of data that allow scholars to explore complex questions, uncover patterns, and generate new insights. This shift from traditional paper-based resources to dynamic digital environments signifies a fundamental rethinking of how research is conducted and knowledge is produced. The integration of databases into humanities research offers numerous opportunities, including enhanced data accessibility, advanced analytical techniques, collaborative research, and innovative pedagogical approaches. These tools enable researchers to examine large-scale data sets and extract meaningful patterns that can inform new interpretations and discoveries. However, this transition also presents challenges such as technical complexity, the digital divide, and data management and preservation. Mastering database technologies requires acquiring technical skills and knowledge, which can be daunting for those accustomed to traditional methods. Addressing the learning curve and providing adequate training is essential for effective implementation. Ensuring equitable access to digital resources and technologies is crucial for inclusive scholarship. Additionally, managing and preserving digital resources poses unique challenges, necessitating ongoing maintenance and thoughtful strategies for data stewardship.

As we embark on this new chapter in humanities scholarship, it is essential to approach database technologies with enthusiasm and critical awareness. The potential for innovation and discovery is immense, but it is equally important to navigate the ethical, practical, and theoretical implications of digital methods. This textbook aims to guide readers through the landscape of databases in the digital humanities, providing foundational knowledge, practical techniques, and illustrative examples. It serves as a valuable resource for students, researchers, and educators, supporting their endeavours to harness the power of digital tools and advance the field of humanities.

In conclusion, the journey from traditional to digital humanities; traditional text reading to data represents a paradigm shift in scholarly practice. By embracing the opportunities offered by databases and addressing the associated challenges, the book unlocks new possibilities for research, teaching, and understanding.

## CHAPTER ONE

Database Theory and Praxis

This chapter explores the notion of a database as an abstract apparatus, representing essential system characteristics without specific implementation intricacies. The objective is to describe the primary elements of a database system, without formal notation or notions related to representation, development, or implementation. This chapter, thus, gives an introduction to these challenges by going through the design and implementation of a simple relational database (e.g., storing basic information about books in print). The objective is to eliminate some of the intricacies and quirks of real-world data so that the technical and conceptual elements of database architecture can more easily emerge. The facts to which humanist academics are used – literary masterpieces, historical events, textual recensions, linguistic occurrences – are seldom straightforward. However, what would be considered as a basic shortcoming has frequently proven to be the principal appeal of relational database systems for the humanist researcher. Contemporary companies often collect and retain data about their everyday operations in an electronic database.

Database: Universe of Discourse (UoD)

Shirley Becker's book *Effective Databases for Text & Document Management* is a comprehensive resource on database management. Other notable works include *Data Mining In Time Series Databases* by Mark Last, Abraham Kandel, and Horst Bunke, *Programming Microsoft Visual Basic.NET for Microsoft Access Databases* by Rick Dobson, *Parallel data mining for very large relational databases* by Freitas A.A., *DBMiner: A System for Data Mining in Relational Databases and Data Warehouses* by Han J., Chiang J.Y., and Chee S., *Methods in Enzymology 411* by David Maier,

Designing SQL Server 2000 Databases for.NET Enterprise Servers by Travis Laird, Robert Patton, and Jennifer Ogle, *The theory of relational databases* by David Maier, *Beginning from Novice to Professional* by Richard Stones, *Multidimensional Databases: Problems and Solutions* [illustrated edition] by Maurizio Rafanelli, *Java persistence for relational databases* by Richard Sperko, and *Communicating with Databases in Natural Language* by Wallace M. provide valuable insights into database management, data mining, and the development of database systems, providing a solid foundation for professionals and students alike. These authors discuss various books and articles on database management systems, data mining in terms of VB 6 Databases, Professional Visual Basic 6 Databases, Modeling Financial Markets with Visual Basic.NET and Databases, Oracle databases on the Web, Oracle In-Focus Series, Mastering Dreamweaver MX databases, and Visual Basic.NET databases. There are other books like *Databases Demystified* by Andrew J. Oppel, *Databases A Beginner's Guide* by Tony Oppel, *Beginning C# 2005 Databases: From Novice to Professional* by James Huddleston, *Designing SQL Server 2000 Databases* by Travis Laird, Robert Patton, and Jennifer Ogle offer a comprehensive overview of database systems, their foundations, their applications in various fields, and valuable insights into database development and management. The problem is that they do not provide information on how to work with databases in humanities and social sciences.

A database represents an organization's reality, sometimes referred to as a universe of discourse (UoD) or domain of discourse. A universe of discourse (UoD), consists of classes and the connections between these classes, which are determined by their qualities or attributes. UoD refers to the specific area or domain of the real world that a database is designed to model. It encompasses all the relevant entities and relationships that the database aims to represent. For instance, if you're creating a database for a university, the UoD would include entities like students, courses, and faculty, along with the relationships between them.

Classes and Relationships

Classes: These are categories or types of entities within the UoD. Each class represents a group of objects with similar characteristics. For example, in a university database, the classes might include students, courses, and professors. Each class is defined by its properties or attributes, such as

Student having attributes like student_id, name, and enrollment_date.

Relationships: These describe how different classes are related to one another. For instance, a Student might be enrolled in multiple Courses, and a Professor might teach several Courses. These relationships can be represented in the database schema to capture the interactions and connections between entities.

Attributes: These are the specific details or properties that define the instances of a class. For example, the Student class may have attributes like student_id, name, and date_of_birth. These attributes help in distinguishing between different instances of a class and storing relevant information about them. By modeling the UoD with classes and relationships, databases help organizations manage and manipulate data efficiently, reflecting real-world processes and interactions.

Database design

Database design is the process of expressing classes, properties, and relationships in a database. A database is a structured compilation of data designed to reflect a certain domain of knowledge, known as the Universe of Discourse (UoD). Data are facts, while information is interpreted data and arranged within a relevant context. Information is data with a given semantics or meaning, and databases establish 'closed worlds' where only what is openly stated is accepted as true. A database is stated to be in a specific condition at a given moment, with a state describing the entire set of facts that are true at a particular point in time. Data in a database is characterized as persistent, meaning it is retained for some length. Persistence is used to differentiate more permanent data from data that is more fleeting in nature. A database is made up of two parts: an intensional portion and an extensional part. The intention of a database is a collection of definitions explaining the structure or organization of a certain database, while the extension is the total set of data in the database. The action of defining a schema for a database system is referred to as database design.

Integrity is a significant element of modern information systems, as most databases are intended to change over time. If a database does not change, it is not an issue of concern. It is important to view database change as happening in discrete rather than continuous time, with some valid states creating the extension of the database at that moment in time. Integrity is the process of guaranteeing that a database travels through a space defined by legitimate states.

Purpose of the database

Databases serve several crucial purposes within organizations and systems. Here's a summary of their main functions:

1. Data Storage and Management

Centralized Storage: Databases provide a centralized location for storing data, making it easier to manage and maintain.

Structured Data Management: They offer structured formats for storing data, which helps in organizing, categorizing, and accessing it efficiently.

2. Data Retrieval

Efficient Access: Databases use indexing and querying mechanisms to allow quick retrieval of data, even from large datasets.

Complex Queries: They support complex queries and searches, enabling users to extract specific information based on various criteria.

3. Data Integrity and Accuracy

Validation Rules: Databases enforce rules and constraints (such as primary keys, foreign keys, and data types) to ensure data integrity and accuracy.

Consistency: They ensure that data remains consistent and accurate across the database, even in cases of concurrent updates.

4. Data Security

Access Control: Databases provide mechanisms for controlling who can access or modify data, ensuring that only authorized users can perform certain actions.

Encryption: Sensitive data can be encrypted to protect it from unauthorized access and breaches.

5. Data Backup and Recovery

Backup Procedures: Databases offer features for regularly backing up data, ensuring that information can be recovered in case of loss or corruption.

Recovery Mechanisms: They include mechanisms to restore data to a previous state, aiding in disaster recovery and business continuity.

6. Data Manipulation

Data Modification: Databases allow for the modification of data through operations such as inserts, updates, and deletes.

Transactional Support: They support transactions, ensuring that modifications are applied atomically, consistently, and durably.

7. Data Sharing and Collaboration

Multi-user Access: Databases enable multiple users to access and work with the data simultaneously, facilitating collaboration and shared use.

Concurrency Control: They manage concurrent data access to prevent conflicts and ensure that users' interactions do not negatively impact data consistency.

8. Data Analysis and Reporting

Data Aggregation: Databases can aggregate data to produce reports, summaries, and analyses.

Business Intelligence: They support tools and queries for business intelligence, helping organizations make informed decisions based on data analysis.

9. Scalability

Handling Growth: Databases are designed to handle increasing volumes of data and users, ensuring performance and usability as organizations grow.

Adaptability: They can be scaled horizontally (across multiple servers) or vertically (by increasing resources on a single server) to meet changing needs.

10. Automation

Scheduled Tasks: Databases support automation of repetitive tasks such as data backups, report generation, and routine maintenance.

Stored Procedures and Triggers: They allow for the creation of stored procedures and triggers to automate complex operations and ensure consistent processing.

Concept of the Database in Digital Humanities

Digital humanities databases are crucial for organizing, managing, and analyzing various data types in humanities research. They store and interact with complex datasets, including textual data, metadata, multimedia data, and spatial data. Database models include relational, document-oriented, graph, and spatial databases. Applications include text analysis, digital editions, GIS mapping, cataloging, and network analysis. Database design considerations include schema design, data integration, and query capabilities. Tools and technologies include database management systems, digital humanities tools, and content management systems. Challenges include data quality, preservation, interdisciplinary collaboration, and ethical issues. Future directions include enhanced interactivity and AI integration.

Database abstraction and three levels

Databases have been a fundamental element of humanistic activity for ages, with the construction of such systems being a cornerstone of humanistic endeavour. The computerized database evolved concurrently with the early usage of computers in academic and commercial sectors, compounding the key challenge of structure and efficient retrieval. The use of database technology among humanists has been revitalized by the discovery that interesting issues and intellectual potential lay underlying these ostensibly practical difficulties.

The most fascinating database work in humanities computing unavoidably launches into less clear ground. Where the business professional may aim to catch airline ticket sales or employee statistics, the humanist researcher tries to capture historical occurrences, encounters between characters, instances of dialectical forms, or editions of books. The most intriguing database work in humanistic research is the interposing of suggestive uncertainty of "was influenced by", "is simultaneous with", "resembles", and "is derived from."

Such interactions hold up the promise not just of an enhanced capacity to retain and retrieve knowledge but also of an increased critical and methodological self-awareness. If the database allows one to home in on information or link rapidly, it also permits the fortuitous connection to come forward. Relational databases in humanistic inquiry are, in this sense, not so much pre-interpretative processes as para-interpretative structures.

Relational database management systems (RDBMS) constitute the most common means of generating searchable ontologies both among computer humanists and among professionals in other fields of study and industry. This chapter will be concerned mostly with the design and implementation of database systems utilizing the relational paradigm.

E. F. Codd initially presented the relational model in a 1970 essay in Communications of the ACM entitled "A Relational Model of Data for Large Shared Databanks." Codd's model made enormous advances ahead in both areas, although his success is arguably more painfully obvious in the mathematical exposition of his concepts. This core notion has inspired a wide literature dedicated to database theory, and although there have been numerous key improvements to the relational model, the relational databases of today continue to work based on Codd's ideas.

Database design is an important part of information management, enabling users to store and retrieve data about a certain subject. For instance, a database may be constructed to collect information about current editions of American books, writers, works, and publishers, enabling users to ask inquiries about the condition of that area. The simplest database would present the data in tabular form, but growing to include a massive collection of authors and works might lead to inefficiencies.

Relational modelling aims to factor these redundancies out of the system by separating specific entities in the domain at a more abstract level. This entails sequestering the different entities according to particular logical groupings: writers (who have last names, first names, and dates of birth and death), works (which have titles and years of publishing), and publishers (which have names and places where they are based). Nouns and verb phrases define the nature of the connections among the entities, such as writers generating works and works being published by publishers.

The entity-relationship (ER) diagram depicts the fundamental linkages we have identified, but it remains to establish how many instances of a single object may be connected with other entities in the model. For example, one author may sign with various publishers, and a publisher may offer many distinct works by several writers. To represent these properties diagrammatically, we may use the number "1" to signify a single occurrence and a "M" to denote multiple instances.

To express the interconnections between records, we need to provide some variable that can retain these links. This may be performed by referring to each instance of a certain thing as a unique datum. The final database will not merely link writers to works in some basic manner but will represent the fact that, for example, the author Mark Twain authored both Huckleberry Finn and Tom Sawyer. The conventional approach for creating this uniqueness is to construct a primary key for each record, which is a unique value linked with each particular entry in a database. This value is merely a new attribute which may be added to the ER diagram and by extension, a new column in the final database for each record type.

Hence, database design is vital for information management, especially in the world of databases. By separating individual entities and using relational modeling, we may increase the efficiency and correctness of our database. By resolving the redundancies present in the original design and embracing the unique properties of each object, we may construct a more efficient and effective database system.

Advantages and disadvantages of databases

As said earlier, a database system offers numerous advantages, including reducing data redundancy, controlling inconsistency, facilitating data sharing, enforcing standards, ensuring data security, and maintaining integrity. It also facilitates data sharing, enforces standards, and ensures data security, making it a valuable tool for managing and enhancing data.

1. Reduces Database Data Redundancy to a Great Extent

Centralized Data Storage: By storing data in a central repository, databases eliminate the need for multiple copies of the same data across different systems or departments.

Normalization: Databases use normalization techniques to organize data efficiently, breaking it into related tables to minimize redundancy. This ensures that each piece of data is stored only once.

Consistency: Reducing redundancy helps maintain data consistency, as changes need to be made in only one place rather than across multiple records.

2. The Database Can Control Data Inconsistency to a Great Extent

Single Source of Truth: With centralized storage, there is a single version of each piece of data, reducing the likelihood of inconsistencies that arise from multiple versions.

Data Integrity Constraints: Databases enforce integrity constraints (e.g., primary keys, foreign keys) to ensure that data adheres to specified rules, preventing inconsistent or invalid data entries.

Automatic Updates: Changes to data are reflected in real-time across all related records, reducing the risk of discrepancies.

3. The Database Facilitates Sharing of Data

Multi-user Access: Databases allow multiple users to access and work with the data concurrently, facilitating collaboration and information sharing within an organization.

Controlled Access: Permissions and roles can be assigned to manage who can view, modify, or delete data, ensuring that data is shared appropriately and securely.

Integration: Databases can be integrated with other systems and applications, allowing seamless data sharing across different platforms and services.

4. Databases Enforce Standards

Data Definition Standards: Databases use standardized data types and schemas to define how data is stored, ensuring consistency in how data is represented and managed.

Naming Conventions: Enforcing naming conventions and data standards helps maintain uniformity in database objects (tables, columns, etc.), making the database easier to understand and manage.

Transaction Standards: Databases adhere to standard transaction protocols (ACID properties) to ensure reliable and predictable processing of data operations.

5. The Database Can Ensure Data Security

Access Controls: Databases implement access control mechanisms to restrict who can access or modify data. This includes user authentication, authorization, and role-based permissions.

Encryption: Sensitive data can be encrypted both at rest and in transit to protect it from unauthorized access or breaches.

Audit Trails: Databases often provide audit trails and logs to track data access and modifications, helping in monitoring and identifying any unauthorized activities.

6. Integrity Can Be Maintained Through Databases

Data Integrity Constraints: The database enforces constraints like primary keys (unique identifiers for records) and foreign keys (relationships between tables) to ensure data integrity.

Validation Rules: They apply validation rules to ensure that data meets certain criteria before being entered into the database, reducing errors and inconsistencies.

Referential Integrity: By enforcing referential integrity, databases ensure that relationships between data are consistent and that foreign key references point to valid records.

Database systems are preferred for their superior performance and efficiency due to their ability to address key data management issues, such as redundancy reduction, control inconsistency, sharing facilitation, standard enforcement, security, and integrity, thereby enhancing decision-making and operational effectiveness within organizations.

Disadvantages of Database Systems

Database systems offer advantages such as efficient data management, data independence, future development, and structured data organization. However, they also have disadvantages such as potential security and integrity issues, extra hardware requirements, performance overhead, optimization needs, and system complexity. To address these drawbacks, it is essential to implement good practices in database management, security, and performance optimization. Addressing these drawbacks requires implementing good practices in database management, security, and performance optimization to ensure the system meets organizational needs effectively. I add here that a database is a structured collection of interrelated data stored together to serve multiple applications. It provides a controlled way to add, modify, and retrieve data, ensuring data independence from the programs that use it.

Purpose and Benefits

Efficient Data Management: Databases allow for organized and efficient management of data, supporting decision-making and application development.

Data Independence: Data is stored in a way that is independent of the applications that use it, enabling flexibility in how data is accessed and manipulated.

Future Development: The structured data organization supports future application development and integration, facilitating scalability and adaptability.

Controlled Approach

Data Handling: Databases use controlled approaches to data handling, including standardized methods for data insertion, modification, and retrieval.

Structured Data: Data is organized in a structured manner to ensure consistency and reliability, providing a foundation for both current and future application needs.

Disadvantages

Databases are essential tools for managing and organizing data, but they have several disadvantages. These include complexity, cost, performance issues, data security, privacy, data integrity, maintenance and upgrades, dependency on specific technologies, resource requirements, data migration and integration, and complexity in distributed databases. Addressing these challenges requires careful planning, skilled administration, and investing in additional tools or technologies. Despite these challenges, databases remain essential for modern data management, but they require careful planning, skilled administration, and the ability to learn effectively.

Security May Be Compromised Without Good Controls

Risk of Unauthorized Access: Without robust security measures, databases are vulnerable to unauthorized access, which can lead to data breaches.

Complex Security Management: Ensuring security involves managing user permissions, encryption, and regular security audits. Poorly implemented security controls can expose sensitive data.

Evolving Threats: Security threats are constantly evolving, so continuous updates and monitoring are necessary to protect against new vulnerabilities.

Integrity May Be Compromised Without Good Controls

Data Integrity Issues: Without proper constraints and validation rules, the integrity of data can be compromised. This includes issues like duplicate records or invalid data entries.

Lack of Referential Integrity: Failing to enforce referential integrity can lead to orphaned records or inconsistent data relationships.

Data Entry Errors: Inadequate validation and control mechanisms can result in incorrect data being entered into the database.

Extra Hardware May Be Required

Increased Resource Needs: Databases, especially large or complex ones, may require additional hardware resources such as high-performance servers, storage systems, and backup solutions.

Scalability Concerns: As data volumes grow, additional hardware may be necessary to maintain performance and accommodate increased load.

Performance Overhead May Be Significant

Resource Consumption: Running complex queries, maintaining indexes, and processing large volumes of data can impose significant performance overhead on database systems.

Optimization Needs: Database performance often requires tuning and optimization, which can be time-consuming and require specialized expertise.

Concurrency Issues: Managing multiple simultaneous users and transactions can impact performance and require advanced concurrency control mechanisms.

The System Is Likely to Be Complex

Complex Architecture: Modern database systems can have intricate architectures, including distributed systems, replication setups, and complex schemas.

Management Complexity: Managing a database involves various tasks such as schema design, backup and recovery, performance tuning, and security management, which can be complex and require specialized knowledge.

User Training: Users and administrators need to be trained to effectively use and manage the database system, adding to the complexity.

While database systems offer significant advantages in managing and utilizing data, they also come with certain challenges and disadvantages, such as potential security and integrity issues, extra hardware requirements, performance overhead, and system complexity. Addressing these drawbacks involves implementing good practices in database management, security, and performance optimization to ensure the database system meets organizational needs effectively.

Object-based and AI-based databases

Object-based and AI-based databases are different approaches to data management. Object-based databases store data in the form of objects, similar to object-oriented programming. They offer advantages like hierarchical structure, support for complex data types, and seamless integration with object-oriented programming languages. AI-based databases use artificial intelligence and machine learning to enhance data management, analytics, querying, and automation. Examples include IBM DB2 with AI, Microsoft Azure SQL Database with AI features, and Oracle Autonomous Database. Let's understand clearly how Object-based and AI-based databases represent different paradigms and approaches to data management.

Object-Based Databases

Object-based databases (also known as object-oriented databases) store data in the form of objects, similar to the way objects are used in object-oriented programming (OOP). This model aligns closely with object-oriented programming principles and provides several advantages:

Object-Oriented Structure

Data Representation: Objects in the database represent real-world entities with attributes (properties) and methods (functions) that operate on these attributes.

Inheritance: Objects can inherit properties and methods from other objects, allowing for a hierarchical structure and reuse of common code.

Complex Data Types

Rich Data Models: Object-based databases support complex data types and structures, including nested objects, arrays, and collections, which can represent intricate real-world scenarios more naturally.

Encapsulation: Data and the methods that operate on the data are encapsulated within objects, promoting modularity and reusability.

Seamless Integration with OOP

Programming Integration: They integrate well with object-oriented programming languages like Java, C++, and Python, making it easier to map objects in code to database entities without requiring complex translation.

Support for Custom Data Types

Flexibility: Users can define custom data types and methods tailored to specific application requirements, offering greater flexibility in data modelling.

Examples: Examples of object-based databases include ObjectDB, db4o, and Versant Object Database.

AI-Based Databases

AI-based databases leverage artificial intelligence (AI) and machine learning (ML) technologies to enhance data management, retrieval, and analysis. These databases integrate AI techniques to provide advanced functionalities:

Enhanced Data Analytics

Predictive Analytics: AI-based databases can analyze historical data to make predictions about future trends and behaviours, aiding in decision-making.

Pattern Recognition: They can identify patterns and correlations in large datasets that might be difficult for traditional databases to uncover.

Intelligent Querying

Natural Language Processing (NLP): AI-based databases can use NLP to allow users to interact with the database using natural language queries, making data retrieval more intuitive.

Semantic Search: AI algorithms can understand the context and semantics of queries to provide more relevant search results.

Automation and Optimization

Automated Maintenance: AI can automate routine database maintenance tasks, such as performance tuning, backups, and data cleaning.

Anomaly Detection: AI can detect anomalies and outliers in data, which can be crucial for fraud detection, system monitoring, and quality control.

Adaptive Learning

Learning from Data: AI-based databases can adapt and improve their performance over time by learning from the data they process and the queries they handle. AI-based database technologies include, for example, IBM Db2 with AI, Microsoft Azure SQL Database with AI features, and Oracle Autonomous Database.

Hence, Object-Based Databases focus on modelling data in a way that mirrors object-oriented programming principles, offering advantages in handling complex data structures and integrating with object-oriented languages. AI-Based Databases incorporate artificial intelligence and machine learning to enhance data analytics, querying, and automation, providing more advanced capabilities for data management and analysis. However, both approaches represent advancements in database technology, catering to different needs and use cases in data management.

Data Breach and Leakage

Data breaches and leakage are significant issues in database management, involving unauthorized access to sensitive information. Causes include cyberattacks, phishing, malware, insider threats, weak security controls, and physical security breaches. Financial loss, reputation damage, and legal and compliance issues can result from breaches. Data leakage involves unauthorized or unintentional transmission of data from within an organization to an external recipient or system. Mitigation strategies include strict access controls, encryption, regular security audits, compliance checks, user education and training, monitoring and response, data classification and handling policies, and regular updates and patching. By understanding these issues and implementing robust security measures, organizations can better protect their databases and sensitive information.

Data Breach

A data breach occurs when unauthorized individuals gain access to sensitive, protected, or confidential data. This can result in data theft, unauthorized use, or exposure of the information.

Causes of Data Breaches

Data breaches can occur due to various factors, including cybersecurity threats, technical vulnerabilities, human errors, insider threats, physical security breaches, third-party risks, social engineering, network attacks, data transfer and storage issues, legal and compliance failures, advanced persistent threats (APTs), and cloud security issues. To mitigate the risk of data breaches, organizations should implement robust security measures, conduct regular security training, monitor and respond to potential breaches, secure third-party relationships, and adhere to compliance standards. By understanding and addressing these causes, organizations can better protect their data and minimize the risk of breaches.

Cyberattacks

Hacking: Attackers exploit vulnerabilities in database systems or applications to gain unauthorized access.

Phishing: Attackers use deceptive emails or messages to trick users into revealing login credentials or other sensitive information.

Malware: Malicious software can compromise database security by infecting systems and stealing data.

Insider Threats

Malicious Insiders: Employees or contractors intentionally misuse their access to steal or damage data.

Negligent Insiders: Employees accidentally expose data through careless actions, such as improper handling or sharing of sensitive information.

Weak Security Controls

Poor Access Management: Inadequate control over who can access sensitive data can lead to unauthorized access.

Unpatched Vulnerabilities: Failure to apply security patches or updates can leave databases open to exploitation.

Physical Security Breaches

Theft of Devices: Physical theft of devices containing sensitive data can result in data breaches if the data is not properly secured.

Consequences of Data Breaches

Financial Loss: Costs associated with managing the breach, legal penalties, and compensation to affected individuals.

Reputation Damage: Loss of customer trust and damage to the organization's reputation.

Legal and Compliance Issues: Potential fines and legal actions for failing to protect sensitive data according to regulations.

Data Leakage

Data leakage refers to the unauthorized or unintentional transmission of data from within an organization to an external recipient or system. This can occur without malicious intent or may result from improper handling of data.

Causes of Data Leakage

Data leakage is the unauthorized or unintended exposure of sensitive information, often resulting from inadvertent actions or systemic weaknesses. Common causes include human error, inadequate security measures, insufficient access controls, device and media loss, poor data management practices, inadequate training and awareness, misconfigured systems, insider threats, external threats, software vulnerabilities, third-party risks, and ineffective data disposal. To mitigate the risk, organizations should implement strong security measures, provide regular employee training, conduct regular audits, secure devices and media, and manage third-party risks. By understanding and addressing these causes, organizations can better protect sensitive information and reduce the risk of data leakage.

Accidental Sharing

Misconfigured Settings: Incorrect configuration of database access controls or data sharing settings can lead to unintended exposure of data.

Human Error: Employees might accidentally send sensitive data to the wrong recipients or upload it to unsecured locations.

Weak Encryption

Unencrypted Data: Data that is not encrypted can be easily accessed if intercepted or accessed by unauthorized individuals.

Uncontrolled Data Access

Permissive Access: Providing excessive access rights to users or applications can lead to unauthorized data exposure or leakage.

Insecure Data Storage and Transmission:

Unprotected Storage: Storing data in insecure or unencrypted formats increases the risk of leakage.

Insecure Communication Channels: Using insecure communication channels (e.g., unencrypted email) can lead to data being intercepted during transmission.

Consequences of Data Leakage

Compliance Violations: Failure to protect data can result in non-compliance with regulations such as GDPR, HIPAA, or CCPA.

Loss of Competitive Advantage: Sensitive business information or intellectual property leakage can harm the organization's competitive position.

Customer Trust Issues: Leakage of customer data can erode trust and lead to customer churn.

Mitigating Data Breaches and Leakage

Implement Strong Security Controls

Access Management: It enforces strict access controls. It ensures that only authorized individuals have access to sensitive data.

Encryption: Use strong encryption methods for data at rest and in transit to protect against unauthorized access.

Regular Security Audits

Vulnerability Assessments: Regular security audits conduct regular security assessments and penetration testing to identify and address vulnerabilities.

Compliance Checks: Ensure adherence to data protection regulations and industry standards.

User Education and Training

Security Awareness: Train employees on security best practices, recognizing phishing attempts, and proper handling of sensitive data.

Monitor and Respond

Intrusion Detection: Implement intrusion detection and prevention systems to identify and respond to potential breaches in real time.
Incident Response Plan: Develop and maintain an incident response plan to manage and mitigate the impact of data breaches or leaks.

Data Classification, Patch Handling Policies

Data Classification

Categorize data based on sensitivity and apply appropriate security measures according to its classification.

Secure Handling Procedures

Establish procedures for securely handling, storing, and transmitting sensitive data.

Patch Management

Apply security patches and updates promptly to address known vulnerabilities in database systems and applications.

Conclusion and Recommendations

Hence, the chapter illustrated the theory and praxis of databases as two complementary aspects of database management. It presented how Database theory focuses on the foundational principles, models, and algorithms of database systems, while practice involves the practical application of these principles in real-world scenarios. Key concepts include relational models, entity-relationship models, object-oriented models, normalization, query languages, transactions, concurrency control, indexing, and data integrity. Database practice includes database design, implementation, administration, security, access control, maintenance, and emerging technologies like NoSQL and cloud databases.

## CHAPTER TWO

Development of Database

Introduction: Development of Dataset

The development of databases (Adam; Blasgen) has evolved significantly over the past few decades, driven by advancements in technology and changes in data management needs. Key stages include early data management (1950s-1960s), which used hierarchical models, network models, relational databases (1970s-1980s), object-oriented and object-relational databases (1980s-1990s), no-sql databases (2000s-present), new-sql databases (2010s-present), and cloud-based databases (2010s-present).

Early database systems used hierarchical models

Early database systems used hierarchical models, which were rigid and inflexible, making it difficult to adapt to changing data needs. Network databases, (Camurcuoglu) developed in the late 1960s, allowed for more complex relationships between data elements, making them more flexible but still complex to manage and query. Relational databases,(Stout, Quentin and Patricia) introduced by Edgar F. Codd in 1970, represented data in tables with rows and columns, simplifying data management by using SQL.

Object-oriented and object-relational databases (1980s-1990s)

Object-oriented and object-relational databases (1980s-1990s) store data as objects, supporting complex data types and relationships.

No-SQL and New SQL databases (2000s-present)

No-SQL databases (2000s-present) store data as documents, key-value stores, column-family stores, and graph databases. New SQL databases aim to combine the scalability and performance advantages of NoSQL systems with the reliability and consistency of traditional SQL databases.

Cloud-based databases

Cloud-based databases, hosted on cloud platforms, offer scalability and cost-effectiveness, reducing the need for on-premises hardware and providing a pay-as-you-go pricing model. Future trends include big data and analytics integration, AI integration, and distributed databases. (Camurcuoglu)

MariaDB

Introduction

MariaDB is a popular open-source relational database management system (RDBMS) that is a fork of MySQL. It is known for its high performance, robustness, and open-source nature. Creating a database in MariaDB is a fundamental task that sets the stage for organizing and managing data. This guide provides a step-by-step overview of how to make a database in MariaDB.

Prerequisites

MariaDB Server Installation: Ensure that MariaDB server is installed and running on your system.

Installing MariaDB on macOS

Using Homebrew

Step 1: Install Homebrew if not already installed:

```
/bin/bash -c "$(curl -fsSL https://raw.githubusercontent.com/Homebrew/install/HEAD/install.sh)"
```

```bash
/bin/bash -c "$(curl -fsSL https://raw.githubusercontent.com/Home
```

Step 2: Install MariaDB:

```bash
brew install mariadb
```

Step 3: Start MariaDB:

```bash
brew services start mariadb
```

Step 4: Secure the installation (optional but recommended):

```bash
mysql_secure_installation
```

Step 5: Verify the installation:

```bash
mysql -u root -p
```

Figure 1 Install Homebrew

Installing MariaDB on Windows

Using the MariaDB Installer:

Step 1: Download the MariaDB installer from the MariaDB website.

Step 2: Run the installer and follow the setup wizard:

Choose the components you want to install (e.g., MariaDB Server, MariaDB Client).

Configure the server (set the root password and other settings).
Step 3: Complete the installation.
Step 4: Verify the installation:
Open the MariaDB Command Line Client from the Start menu.
Enter the root password you set during installation.

Post-Installation Steps

Regardless of the operating system, it is good practice to:
Secure MariaDB:
Run the mysql_secure_installation command to set up security options like root password, removing anonymous users, disallowing root login remotely, and removing test databases.
Configure MariaDB:
Edit the MariaDB configuration file if needed. The configuration file is usually located at /etc/mysql/my.cnf or /etc/my.cnf on Linux, /usr/local/etc/my.cnf on macOS, and C:\Program Files\MariaDB 10.x\data\my.ini on Windows.
Start and Stop MariaDB:
Linux: Use sudo systemctl start mariadb and sudo systemctl stop mariadb.
macOS: Use brew services start mariadb and brew services stop mariadb.
Windows: Use the Services app or net start mariadb and net stop mariadb from the command prompt.
By following these steps, you can successfully install and configure MariaDB on your preferred operating system.
Create database command
Access Rights: You need to have administrative or appropriate privileges to create databases.

Step-by-Step Process

Access MariaDB Command-Line Interface (CLI):
Open a terminal or command prompt.
Log in to MariaDB using the mysql command-line tool. You will need to provide the root password or the password for a user with sufficient privileges:
mysql -u root -p

Enter your password when prompted.

Create a Database:

Once logged in, you can create a new database using the CREATE DATABASE statement after the update. See syntax in the given Figure:

1. **Update Package Index**

2. **Install MariaDB Server**

3. **Secure MariaDB Installation**

   After installation, you should run the security script to set a root password and secure your installation.

Figure 2 Create database

Follow the prompts to set up your security preferences.

Step 2: Access MariaDB

1. **Log in to MariaDB**

Enter the root password you set up during the security configuration.

Step 3: Create a Database

1. **Create a Database**
   In the MariaDB prompt, use the `CREATE DATABASE` command to create a new database.

   Replace `my_database` with your desired database name.

2. **Verify Database Creation**
   List all databases to confirm creation.

Step 4: Create a User and Grant Privileges

1. **Create a New User**

Figure 3: Create Database-Security Preference

Replace my_user and my_password with your desired username and password.

2. **Grant Privileges to the User**

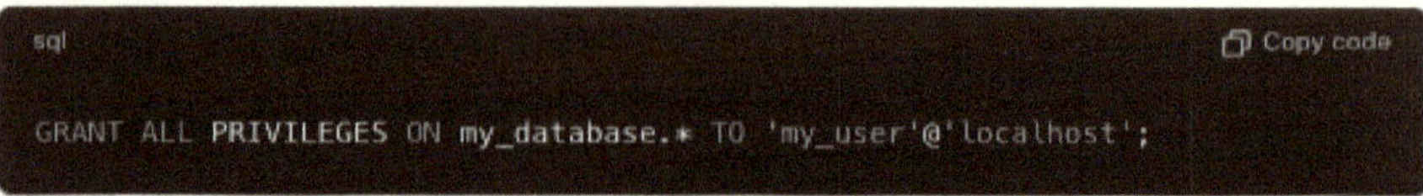

This command grants all privileges on `my_database` to `my_user`.

3. **Flush Privileges**

Step 5: Create Tables and Insert Data

1. **Select the Database**

```sql
USE my_database;
```

2. **Create a Table**

```sql
CREATE TABLE my_table (
    id INT AUTO_INCREMENT PRIMARY KEY,
    name VARCHAR(100),
    created_at TIMESTAMP DEFAULT CURRENT_TIMESTAMP
);
```

3. **Insert Data into the Table**

Figure 4: Inserting Data

Further, execute the query command:

4. **Query Data**

Step 6: Exit MariaDB

1. **Exit the MariaDB Shell**

Step 7: Backup and Restore (Optional)

1. **Backup a Database**

2. **Restore a Database**

Figure 5: Query Data

These are the basic steps to create and manage a database in MariaDB. Verification with show databases

Select the Database:

- To start using the newly created database, you need to select it with the `USE` command:

```sql
USE my_database;
```

Create Tables and Manage Data:

- After selecting the database, you can proceed to create tables and manage data within it. For example, to create a table within `my_database`, you would use:

```sql
CREATE TABLE example_table (
    id INT AUTO_INCREMENT PRIMARY KEY,
    name VARCHAR(255) NOT NULL,
    created_at TIMESTAMP DEFAULT CURRENT_TIMESTAMP
);
```

Figure 6: Verification with Show Database Command

Selecting database with USE command

Additional Considerations: Naming Conventions: Follow proper naming conventions for databases, tables, and columns to clarify and avoid conflicts.

Character Set and Collation: You can specify character set and collation for the database if needed. For instance:

```sql
CREATE DATABASE my_database
CHARACTER SET utf8mb4
COLLATE utf8mb4_general_ci;
```

Figure 7: Selecting database with USE command

MariaDB alter database

Altering a database in MariaDB involves changing its configuration, such as modifying its character set or collation settings. While MariaDB does not support altering certain aspects of a database schema directly (like changing the name of a database), you can modify the character set and collation, which can be necessary for internationalization or performance tuning.

See the instructions on how you can alter a database in MariaDB:

1. Alter Database Character Set and Collation

To change a database's character set and collation, use the ALTER DATABASE statement. This can be useful to ensure that the database handles character data correctly for different languages or special characters.

Figure 8: New Character Set

To change the character set of a database named my_database to utf8mb4 and the collation to utf8mb4_unicode_ci, you would use:

Figure 9: Alter database

2. Alter Database Properties via GUI Tools

If you are using a graphical interface like HeidiSQL or phpMyAdmin, you can also alter the database properties through the GUI.

In HeidiSQL:

Connect to the Database:

Open HeidiSQL and connect to your MariaDB server.

Select the Database:

In the left sidebar, select the database you want to alter.

Open Database Properties:

Right-click on the database name and choose "Alter database" (in some versions, you may need to go to the "Database" menu and select "Alter database").

Modify Character Set and Collation:

Change the character set and collation as needed.

Click "OK" or "Save" to apply the changes.

In phpMyAdmin:

Access phpMyAdmin:

Open phpMyAdmin in your web browser.

Select the Database:

Click on the database you want to modify from the left sidebar.

Open Database Operations:

Click on the "Operations" tab at the top of the page.

Modify Character Set and Collation:

Under the "Collation" section, you can choose a new collation for your database.

phpMyAdmin does not allow direct changes to the character set from the operations tab, but you can use SQL queries in the "SQL" tab to run the ALTER DATABASE command as described above.

3. *Considerations and Limitations*

Table-Level Changes: Changing the database's character set or collation does not automatically alter the character set or collation of existing tables or columns within that database. You will need to use ALTER TABLE statements to change these properties for individual tables and columns if needed.

For example, to alter a table's character set:

```
ALTER TABLE table_name
CONVERT TO CHARACTER SET utf8mb4
COLLATE utf8mb4_unicode_ci;
```

Backup: Always back up your database before making significant changes to avoid accidental data loss.

Impact on Existing Data: Changing the character set or collation might impact existing data, especially if the new settings are not compatible with the existing data.

By following these steps, you can effectively alter your MariaDB database to suit your needs, whether through SQL commands or graphical tools.

MySQL drop database

Dropping a database in MySQL (and MariaDB) is a straightforward process that involves using the DROP DATABASE SQL command. This operation will permanently remove the database and all its contents, including tables, data, indexes, and other objects. Use this command with caution, as this action cannot be undone.

Steps to Drop a Database in MySQL

1. Using the MySQL Command-Line Interface (CLI)

Open the Command-Line Interface:

Open a terminal (Linux/macOS) or Command Prompt (Windows).

Log in to MySQL:

Use the mysql command to log in to the MySQL server. Replace root with your username if necessary, and provide your password when prompted:

mysql -u root -p

Drop the Database:

After logging in, use the DROP DATABASE SQL command to remove the database. Replace database_name with the name of the database you want to drop:

DROP DATABASE database_name;

Verify Deletion:

To ensure the database has been deleted, list all databases with:

SHOW DATABASES;

The dropped database should no longer appear in the list.

Exit the CLI:

To exit the MySQL CLI, type:

EXIT;

2. Using phpMyAdmin

Access phpMyAdmin:

Open phpMyAdmin in your web browser.

Select the Database:

In the left sidebar, click on the database you want to delete.

Drop the Database:

Click on the "Operations" tab at the top of the page.

Scroll down to the "Remove database" section.

Click the "Drop the database (DROP)" link.

Confirm Deletion:

phpMyAdmin will ask you to confirm the deletion. Confirm the action to proceed.

The database and all its contents will be permanently removed.

3. Using HeidiSQL

Open HeidiSQL:

Launch the HeidiSQL application on your computer.

Connect to MySQL:

If you haven't already connected, create a new session and log in to your MySQL server.

Select the Database:

In the left sidebar, locate and select the database you want to drop.

Drop the Database:

Right-click on the database name and choose "Drop database" from the context menu.

A confirmation dialog will appear. Confirm the action to proceed.

Verify Deletion:

Refresh the database list to ensure the database has been removed.

Additional Considerations

Backup: Always back up your database before dropping it. This ensures you can recover data if needed. Use the *mysqldump* command or a graphical tool to create a backup.

Permissions: Ensure you have the necessary permissions to drop the database. You must be logged in as a user with sufficient privileges (e.g., root or a user with DROP permissions).

Impact: Dropping a database is a permanent action. Ensure that the database is no longer needed and that all important data has been backed up or migrated.

Following these steps, you can drop a database in MySQL using various methods, depending on your preference and environment.

Verify Deletion:

To ensure the database has been deleted, list all databases with:

Further, let us have some basics of Python MySQL database creation.

Python MySQL database

Using Python to interact with a MySQL database involves several key steps, including setting up the database connection, executing SQL queries, and managing the results. Here's a comprehensive guide on how to work with MySQL databases in Python:

1. Install Required Libraries

Figure 10: Installing Required Libraries

To work with MySQL in Python, you'll need a MySQL connector library. The most commonly used library is mysql-connector-python or PyMySQL. You can install these libraries using pip:

Using mysql-connector-python

2. Connect to the MySQL Database

You need to establish a connection to your MySQL database using the connector library. Here's how to do it with both mysql-connector-python and PyMySQL.

Using mysql-connector-python:

```python
import mysql.connector

# Establishing the connection
conn = mysql.connector.connect(
    host="localhost",
    user="yourusername",
    password="yourpassword",
    database="yourdatabase"
)


# Creating a cursor object
cursor = conn.cursor()
```

Figure 11: Installing Required Libraries

Using PyMySQL:

```python
import pymysql

# Establishing the connection
conn = pymysql.connect(
    host="localhost",
    user="yourusername",
    password="yourpassword",
    database="yourdatabase"
)

# Creating a cursor object
cursor = conn.cursor()
```

Figure 12: Using PyMySQL

3. Execute SQL Queries

With the connection and cursor set up, you can execute SQL queries. Here are examples of executing different types of queries:

Creating a Table:

Creating a Table:

```python
create_table_query = """
CREATE TABLE employees (
    id INT AUTO_INCREMENT PRIMARY KEY,
    name VARCHAR(100),
    position VARCHAR(100),
    hire_date DATE
)
"""

cursor.execute(create_table_query)
```

Inserting Data:

```python
insert_query = """
INSERT INTO employees (name, position, hire_date)
VALUES (%s, %s, %s)
"""

values = ("John Doe", "Software Engineer", "2024-08-12")
cursor.execute(insert_query, values)
conn.commit()  # Commit the transact
```

Figure 13: Creating Table

Querying Data:

```python
select_query = "SELECT * FROM employees"
cursor.execute(select_query)
results = cursor.fetchall()

for row in results:
    print(row)
```

Updating Data:

```python
update_query = """
UPDATE employees
SET position = %s
WHERE name = %s
"""
values = ("Senior Software Engineer", "John Doe")
cursor.execute(update_query, values)
conn.commit()  # Commit the transaction
```

Figure 14: Querying Data

Deleting Data:

```python
delete_query = "DELETE FROM employees WHERE name = %s"
value = ("John Doe",)
cursor.execute(delete_query, value)
conn.commit()  # Commit the transaction
```

Figure 15: Deleting Data

4. Close the Connection

After performing all necessary operations, make sure to close the cursor and connection to free up resources.

cursor.close()

conn.close()

Additional Considerations on SQL Syntax

Error Handling: Implement error handling to manage exceptions such as connection errors or SQL syntax errors. Use try and except blocks to handle these errors gracefully.

```python
try:
    # Code to connect and perform operations
except mysql.connector.Error as err:
    print(f"Error: {err}")
```

Figure 16: Implementing error handling

Transactions: Use transactions (conn.commit()) to ensure data integrity, especially when performing multiple related operations. If an error occurs, you can roll back the transaction (conn.rollback()).

Security: Avoid hardcoding sensitive information like database passwords. Use environment variables or configuration files for secure management. Following these steps, you can efficiently interact with a MySQL database using Python, allowing you to perform various database operations programmatically.

Text-Oriented Database

Text-Oriented Database Management (TDBM) is a concept developed by Anne Permaloff and Carl Grafton to improve the management, search, and analysis of text data within databases. TDBM systems focus on text data as a central component, handling both unstructured and semi-structured text. They offer enhanced search capabilities, including full-text search, indexing, and semantic search, allowing users to perform complex queries and retrieve relevant text data efficiently.

TDBM systems often use sophisticated methods to represent and organize text data, such as natural language processing (NLP), text normalization, and metadata tagging. These systems integrate seamlessly with text analysis tools, enabling tasks like text mining, sentiment analysis, and topic modelling.

TDBM systems are designed for flexibility and scalability, accommodating varying sizes of text datasets and adapting to different types of textual content. User interfaces are designed to accommodate the needs of those working with text data, including intuitive search and retrieval mechanisms and tools for annotation and managing text.

TDBM systems can handle text in multiple languages, including non-Latin scripts and complex text structures, making them particularly useful for global or multilingual datasets. Contextual awareness features help understand the meaning and relevance of text data based on its context within a document or larger collection.

TDBM's applications include academic and research settings, content management systems, and business intelligence. In academic and research settings, it enables researchers to efficiently locate and analyze relevant information. In content management systems, TDBM enhances the organization and retrieval of large amounts of textual content, improving user experience and accessibility.

Conclusion and Recommendations

To conclude, MariaDB is a robust and versatile relational database management system (RDBMS) that supports a wide range of applications, including those in the social sciences and humanities. Its open-source nature allows for customization and scalability, essential for managing diverse and extensive research data. The active MariaDB community provides valuable support and continuous improvements, aligning well with the collaborative nature of academic research.

MariaDB is compatible with various tools and technologies used in digital humanities and social sciences, including data analysis, visualization, and integration with other systems. Its support for SQL standards and various storage engines enhances its flexibility and adaptability for different research needs. MariaDB incorporates robust security features to protect sensitive research data, which is crucial given the growing concerns about data privacy in academic research.

The system's ability to handle large datasets and complex queries makes it suitable for large-scale research databases, such as those needed for comprehensive bibliometric studies or big data applications in the humanities. Researchers and institutions should consider adopting MariaDB for their database needs, especially when there is a requirement for open-source solutions that offer customization.

To enhance performance and data management, researchers and institutions should leverage the extensive resources and support provided by the MariaDB community, focus on integration capabilities, enhance data security measures, optimize performance for large datasets, explore advanced features, and contribute to the MariaDB community by sharing experiences, developing plugins or extensions, and participating in discussions. By following these conclusions and recommendations, researchers and institutions can effectively utilize MariaDB to support and enhance their work in the social sciences and humanities.

References

Adam, Nabil R. "Special Issue: Database Management." Journal of Management Information Systems, vol. 4, no. 2, 1987, pp. 5–7. JSTOR, http://www.jstor.org/stable/40397862. Accessed 27 Aug. 2024.

Blasgen, Michael W. "Database Systems." Science, vol. 215, no. 4534, 1982, pp. 869–72. JSTOR, http://www.jstor.org/stable/1687482. Accessed 27 Aug. 2024.

Camurcuoğlu, Duygu, et al. "Database." Laying the Foundations: Manual of the British Museum Iraq Scheme Archaeological Training Programme, edited by John MacGinnis and Sebastien Rey, Archaeopress, 2022, pp. 88–96. JSTOR, https://doi.org/10.2307/jj.15136034.14. Accessed 27 Aug. 2024.

Folsom, Ed. "Database as Genre: The Epic Transformation of Archives." PMLA, vol. 122, no. 5, 2007, pp. 1571–79. JSTOR, http://www.jstor.org/stable/25501803. Accessed 27 Aug. 2024.

Hayles, N. Katherine. "Narrative and Database: Natural Symbionts." PMLA, vol. 122, no. 5, 2007, pp. 1603–08. JSTOR, http://www.jstor.org/stable/25501808. Accessed 27 Aug. 2024.

Huse, Charles C. "Database Protection in Theory and Practice: Three Recent Cases." Berkeley Technology Law Journal, vol. 20, no. 1, 2005, pp. 23–45. JSTOR, http://www.jstor.org/stable/24117480. Accessed 27 Aug. 2024.

Permaloff, Anne, and Carl Grafton. "Text-Oriented Database Management." PS: Political Science and Politics, vol. 23, no. 4, 1990, pp. 586–91. JSTOR, https://doi.org/10.2307/419900. Accessed 27 Aug. 2024.

Sipes, James L. "Database Dynamics." Landscape Architecture, vol. 93, no. 3, 2003, pp. 46–91. JSTOR, http://www.jstor.org/stable/44673571. Accessed 27 Aug. 2024.

Stout, Quentin F., and Patricia A. Woodworth. "Relational Databases." The American Mathematical Monthly, vol. 90, no. 2, 1983, pp. 101–18. JSTOR, https://doi.org/10.2307/2975809. Accessed 27 Aug. 2024.

## CHAPTER THREE

DBMS, Models, and Relational Model

DBMS and Database Models

A database is a large collection and integration of data organized for quick search and retrieval, like a computer. A database management system (DBMS) is a suite of libraries, applications, and utilities that relieve application developers from data storage and management details. DBMSs come in various flavours developed over time to solve specific data-storage problems.

Database Models

In the 1960s and 1970s, inventors devised databases that effectively addressed the issue of recurring groups via various approaches. These approaches provide models that are referred to as database system models. The models now in use today are mostly based on research conducted at IBM.

Efficiency was a primary factor that influenced early database system designs. An effective approach to enhance system efficiency was to implement a standardized length for database records, or alternatively, establish a consistent amount of components per record (columns per row). This effectively circumvents the issue of recurring groups. For programmers proficient in any procedural language, it is evident that in this scenario, it is possible to get each record from a database and save it in a simple C structure. Real world is seldom so accommodating, therefore we need to discover strategies to cope with inconveniently formatted data. Database systems designers achieved this by implementing several database classifications.

Hierarchical Database Model

The IMS database system from IBM in the late 1960s established the hierarchical approach for databases. In this concept, assuming data records to be made of collections of others overcomes the repeating groups issue. The model may be likened to a bill of materials used to explain how a complicated manufactured product is made. For example, let's assume an automobile is made of a chassis, a body, an engine, and four wheels. Each of these fundamental components is broken down further. An engine contains some cylinders, a cylinder head, and a crankshaft. These components are broken down further until we come to the nuts and bolts that make up every element in a car. Hierarchical model databases are still in use today, notably Software AG's ADABAS. A hierarchical database system makes it possible to improve data storage to make it more efficient for certain issues; for example, to discover which automotive utilizes a particular component.

Network Database Model

The network model adds the notion of pointers inside the database. Records may include references to other records. So, for example, you may maintain a record for each of your company's consumers. Each client has placed several orders with you over time (a recurring group). The data is organized such that the customer record includes a link to only one order record. Each order record includes both the order data for that particular order and a link to another order record.

A network model database offers certain notable benefits. If you need to discover all of the records of one kind that are connected to a certain record of another type (in this example, the languages spoken in a nation), you may locate them fairly rapidly by following the pointers from the beginning record.

There are, however, some downsides, too. If you wish to list the nations that speak French, you need to follow the connections from all of the country entries, which for huge datasets will be incredibly slow. This can be rectified by having separate linked lists of pointers, particularly for languages, but it fast gets quite complicated and is not a general-purpose solution, because you need to select in advance how the pointers will be created. Writing applications that utilize a network model database may also be highly laborious since the program normally must take responsibility for setting up and maintaining the pointers when entries are changed and destroyed.

Relational Database Model

Relational database management systems (RDBMS) represent the most popular way of creating searchable ontologies among computing humanists and professionals in other areas of research and industry. This chapter will focus primarily on the design and implementation of database systems using the relational model. (Stout, Quentin, and Patricia)

RDBMSs are powerful tools for data management, allowing users to ask questions about stored data in the form of queries. Unlike earlier database designs, relational databases are more flexible, answering questions that were not known at the time of design. Codd's proposals for the relational model suggest that queries might use predicate calculus, a branch of theoretical logic, to provide unprecedented power for searching and selecting data sets. Modern database systems, like PostgreSQL, hide the mathematics behind an expressive and easy-to-learn query language. QUEL, used in the late 1970s Ingres database, was one of the first implementations of a query language. QBE (Query By Example) and SQL (Structured Query Language) were developed around the same time.

SQL and PostgreSQL

SQL is a widely adopted standard for database query languages, defined in international standards. It is used by almost every database system and acts as a good unifier, as applications written to use SQL can be ported to other systems with minimal cost. However, commercial pressures have led to variations in SQL, as the standard does not define commands for many essential database administration tasks.

There are differences between SQL used by Oracle, SQL Server, and PostgreSQL, with PostgreSQL being very close to SQL92: Entry SQL conformance. Developers closely monitor standards compliance, and

PostgreSQL becomes more compliant with each release.

SQL consists of three types of commands: Data Manipulation Language (DML), Data Definition Language (DDL), and Data Control Language (DCL). DML is used 90% of the time for inserting, deleting, updating, and selecting data from the database. DDL is used for creating tables, defining relationships, and controlling other aspects of the database. DCL is used to control permissions on data, such as defining access rights.

Database Management System Responsibilities

A Database Management System (DBMS) is a suite of tools that allow the building of databases and applications. Its tasks include building the database, providing query and update tools, managing multitasking, keeping an audit trail, managing security, and ensuring referential integrity.

DBMSs may handle big files or employ operating system files or raw disk partitions to generate databases. They give essential access to developers and users, ensuring that queries meet particular requirements. Multitasking enables numerous users to access data concurrently without influencing others, allowing for simultaneous readings of data.

DBMSs also maintain an audit trail, retaining track of any modifications to the data for some time. This may be used to examine problems and recreate data in case of system malfunctions, such as unplanned power downs. Data backups and audit trails may be utilized to recover the database in case of disk failure.

Access restrictions guarantee that only authorized users may alter the data housed in the database and its structure. A hierarchy of users is often built for each database, including tools for adding and removing users and designating which features they may use.

Lastly, many database systems preserve referential integrity by notifying errors when a query or change breaches relational model rules. The theory of DBMSs made a tremendous leap forward in 1970 with the publication of "A Relational Model of Data for Large Shared Data Banks," a work by E. F. Codd (see http://www.acm.org/ classics/nov95/toc.html). This seminal work established the notion of relations and illustrated how tables may be used to represent facts that relate to real-world things, and consequently, carry data about them.

By this time, it had also become evident that the primary driving factor behind database design, efficiency, was frequently less significant than another concern: data integrity. The relational model stresses data integrity significantly more than any of the prior approaches. Referential integrity relates to making ensuring that data in the database makes sense at all times, such that, for example, all orders have customers. "Records in a table in a relational database are known as tuples, and this is the terminology you will find used in several areas of the PostgreSQL documentation. A tuple is an ordered set of components, or characteristics, each of which has a specified type.

Stephen Ramsay's "Databases": An Overview

In 1970, E. F. Codd established the relational model to enhance the efficiency of accessing and storing data in large shared databanks. His model made substantial progress in both domains, but his mathematical exposition of his ideas was particularly noteworthy. Codd's concept that a database may be seen as a collection of relations, with each relation being a collection of propositions, facilitated the direct use of formal logic in database access and associated issues. Codd's findings have given rise to an extensive body of literature on database theory, and despite significant advancements, relational databases still rely on these core ideas. In 1970, E. F. Codd's "A Relational Model of Data for Large Shared Data Banks" revolutionized the theory of database management systems (DBMSs). This work introduced the concept of relations and demonstrated how tables can represent facts related to real-world things. The primary focus of database design was often on data integrity, which was emphasized more than efficiency. The relational model emphasizes referential integrity, ensuring that data in the database makes sense at all times.

Stephen Ramsay writes in his article "Databases" that databases have been a significant aspect of humanistic endeavor for centuries, with the development of computerized databases occurring simultaneously with the early use of computers in academic and commercial environments. The computerized database system enables efficient storage and retrieval of information by facilitating interaction with multiple end users, providing platform-independent representations of data, and allowing dynamic insertion and deletion of information. Humanist scholars have been invigorated by the realization that there are fascinating problems and intellectual opportunities beneath these practical matters. Ramsay's introduction to database design and implementation by working through the design and implementation of a simple relational database is huminitic in many senses. He aims to remove some of the complexities and idiosyncrasies of real-world data, allowing the technical and conceptual details of database design to more readily emerge.

He says that the primary attraction of relational database systems for humanist scholars is the ability to increase critical and methodological self-awareness. Relational databases in the humanistic study are not pre-interpretative mechanisms but para-interpretative formations, enabling the act of creation to be as vital to the experiential meaning of the scholarly endeavour as the use of the final product.

Database design of literary arts

A database is a system that stores information about a specific domain, such as the universe of discourse, and allows users to inquire about its current status. For example, a database for American novels would store data about writers, works, and publishers, allowing users to inquire about specific information. The most basic form of a database would consist of a tabular representation of the data.

The potential for expanding this database to include a wide array of writers and literary works is considerable. However, inefficiencies exist in relational models, such as the need to insert the author's name into every row when a new work is introduced. This redundancy also exists with dates of publication, publisher names, and publishing addresses. Changing an author's name also requires updating all areas where the old name occurs.

In addition to redundancy, redundancy can be a significant burden in systems holding hundreds or millions of objects. In this scenario, any computer can make rapid work of a database with six entries. However, in a system holding hundreds or millions of objects, the additional time and space needed to run search algorithms might become a significant burden. Relational modeling is a method used to eliminate redundancies in databases by isolating individual entities in the domain and identifying types of information that vary independently. This process involves creating an entity relationship (ER) diagram, which captures the basic relationships between entities. To represent the relationships between records, a variable can be introduced to hold these connections. A primary key is created for each record, a unique value associated with each record in a table. This value is then added to the ER diagram and a new column in the final database for each record type. A foreign key is introduced to capture the one-to-many (1:M) relationship between authors and works. This method helps to retain one reference for the author Mark Twain and eliminates redundancies. However, redundancies may still appear after a considerable amount of data has been entered into the database.

Schema design

Database design involves translating design into a machine-readable representation called a database schema, created using Structured Query Language (SQL). Popular open-source systems include MySQL, mSQL, and Post-greSQL, while commercial systems like Oracle, Microsoft Access, and IBM DB2 are used. We have already practised in the previous chapter. PostgreSQL, an open-source database system with over 35 years of development, is known for its reliability, robustness, and performance. Students in humanities may use PostgreSQL.

What is PostgreSQL?

PostgreSQL is a relational database management system (DBMS) that supports the SQL standard query language and is capable, reliable and has good performance characteristics. It can run on various UNIX platforms, including FreeBSD, Linux, Mac OS X, Microsoft Windows NT/2000/2003 servers, and even Windows XP for development. PostgreSQL is free and open source offering features similar to commercial or open-source databases, but with some extras. PostgreSQL is a stable database system with strict management and comprehensive testing, allowing for speedy problem patches thanks to its vast user community and universal access to the source code. Its performance has increased with each version, and current benchmarks suggest it may compare well with commercial competitors, while less fully equipped systems may outperform it at lower functionality. Its features include:

1. Relational model for databases

2. SQL standard query language support
3. High performance and reliability
4. Support for various UNIX platforms
5. Free and open source
6. Comparable to other DBMSs with similar features.

Exploration of PostgreSQL

PostgreSQL, a relational database, originated in 1977 at the University of California at Berkeley (UCB) where Ingres was created. It became a popular export and was adopted by Relational Technologies/Ingres Corporation, making it one of the first commercially accessible RDBMSs. Ingres was widely used in academic and research areas. It was developed at UCB from 1986 to 1994 and was later sold to Illustra, a commercial company. In 1994 SQL features were added, and the name was changed to Postgres95. By 1996, Postgres gained popularity, leading to its development being open to a mailing list. The final name change was to "SQL" to reflect its support for the query language standard. Today, a team of internet developers develops it similar to other open-source software like Perl, Apache, and PHP. Users can contribute fixes, enhancements, and suggestions for new features, and official releases are made via *http://www.postgresql.org*.

Installation of PostgreSQL

Installing PostgreSQL involves several steps that vary depending on your operating system. Below is a comprehensive guide to installing PostgreSQL on Windows, macOS, and Linux.

1. Installation on Windows

Using the PostgreSQL Installer
    Download the Installer:
    Go to the PostgreSQL official download page.
    Download the Windows installer from EnterpriseDB.
    Run the Installer:
    Run the downloaded .exe file to start the installation process.
    Follow the Setup Wizard:
    Welcome Screen: Click "Next."

Select Installation Directory: Choose or accept the default directory and click "Next."

Select Components: Ensure "PostgreSQL Server" is selected. You can also choose additional components like pgAdmin.

Data Directory: Choose a directory for your database data and click "Next."

Password: Set the password for the PostgreSQL superuser (default user: postgres).

Port: Choose the port (default is 5432).

Locale: Select your locale or leave it as default.

Ready to Install: Review settings and click "Next" to begin installation.

Installation Progress: Wait for the installation to complete.

Finish: Click "Finish" to exit the setup wizard.

Verify Installation

Open pgAdmin from the Start Menu and connect to the PostgreSQL server using the postgres user and the password you set.

Alternatively, use the command line: Open Command Prompt and type psql -U postgres to access the PostgreSQL interactive terminal.

2. Installation on macOS

Using Homebrew

Install Homebrew (if not already installed):

Open Terminal and run:

/bin/bash -c "$(curl -fsSL https://raw.githubusercontent.com/Homebrew/install/HEAD/install.sh)"

2. **Install PostgreSQL:**

   - Run the following command in Terminal:

3. **Start PostgreSQL Service:**

   - Start the PostgreSQL service with Homebrew:

Figure 1: Installing PostgreSQL

Further, you need to verify the installation.

4. **Verify Installation:**

   - Check the PostgreSQL version:

   - Access the PostgreSQL interactive terminal:

Figure 2: Verifying the installation

Using the PostgreSQL Official Package
Download the Installer:

Go to the PostgreSQL official download page.

Download the macOS installer from EnterpriseDB.

Run the Installer:

Open the .dmg file and run the PostgreSQL installer.

Follow the Setup Wizard:

Welcome Screen: Click "Next."

Installation Directory: Choose or accept the default directory.

Password: Set the password for the PostgreSQL superuser (default user: postgres).

Port: Choose the port (default is 5432).

Locale: Select your locale or leave as default.

Ready to Install: Review settings and click "Next" to begin installation.

Installation Progress: Wait for the installation to complete.

Finish: Click "Finish" to exit the setup wizard.

Verify Installation:

Open Terminal and run: psql -U postgres

Using PostgreSQL for DMLD

Developing and managing literary data (DMLD) is one of the most complex digital humanities activities. It language software-based analysis of texts. Using PostgreSQL for developing and managing literary data involves leveraging its robust features to store, query, and analyze textual and bibliographic information. Here's a comprehensive guide on how to use PostgreSQL effectively for literary data:

1. Setup and Initial Configuration

Install PostgreSQL:

Follow the installation instructions for your operating system as described previously.

Create a Database:

Connect to PostgreSQL using psql or a GUI tool like pgAdmin.

Create a new database for your literary data:

CREATE DATABASE literary_db;

Connect to the Database:

Connect to your new database:

psql -d literary_db

2. Design Your Schema

Designing a schema for literary data involves defining tables and relationships based on the data you want to manage. Common entities in literary data might include books, authors, genres, and reviews.

Example Schema Design:

Authors Table:

```sql
CREATE TABLE authors (
    author_id SERIAL PRIMARY KEY,
    first_name VARCHAR(100),
    last_name VARCHAR(100),
    birth_date DATE,
    nationality VARCHAR(100)
);
```

Genres Table:

```sql
CREATE TABLE genres (
    genre_id SERIAL PRIMARY KEY,
    genre_name VARCHAR(100) UNIQUE
);
```

Books Table:

```sql
CREATE TABLE books (
    book_id SERIAL PRIMARY KEY,
    title VARCHAR(255),
    publication_date DATE,
    author_id INT REFERENCES authors(author_id),
    genre_id INT REFERENCES genres(genre_id),
    isbn VARCHAR(20) UNIQUE
);
```

Figure 3: Author Table Creation

After that, you have to review the table.

4. **Reviews Table:**

```sql
CREATE TABLE reviews (
    review_id SERIAL PRIMARY KEY,
    book_id INT REFERENCES books(book_id),
    reviewer_name VARCHAR(100),
    review_text TEXT,
    rating INT CHECK (rating >= 1 AND rating <= 5),
    review_date DATE
);
```

Figure 4: Review Table

3. *Populate the Tables*

Insert data into your tables using the INSERT INTO command. Let us have an example:

1. **Insert Authors:**

```sql
INSERT INTO authors (first_name, last_name, birth_date, nationality)
VALUES ('Jane', 'Austen', '1775-12-16', 'British');
```

2. **Insert Genres:**

```sql
INSERT INTO genres (genre_name)
VALUES ('Fiction'), ('Romance');
```

3. **Insert Books:**

```sql
INSERT INTO books (title, publication_date, author_id, genre_id, isbn)
VALUES ('Pride and Prejudice', '1813-01-28', 1, 1, '978-0141040349');
```

4. **Insert Reviews:**

```sql
INSERT INTO reviews (book_id, reviewer_name, review_text, rating, review_date)
VALUES (1, 'John Doe', 'A timeless classic with wit and charm.', 5, '2024-08-12
```

Figure 5: Populate Table

4. Query the Data

Perform queries to retrieve and analyze your literary data. Example Queries

```sql
SELECT b.title, b.publication_date
FROM books b
JOIN authors a ON b.author_id = a.author_id
WHERE a.last_name = 'Austen';
```

Get All Reviews for a Specific Book:

```sql
SELECT r.reviewer_name, r.review_text, r.rating
FROM reviews r
JOIN books b ON r.book_id = b.book_id
WHERE b.title = 'Pride and Prejudice';
```

Count Books by Genre:

```sql
SELECT g.genre_name, COUNT(b.book_id) AS num_books
FROM genres g
LEFT JOIN books b ON g.genre_id = b.genre_id
GROUP BY g.genre_name;
```

Find High-Rated Books:

```sql
SELECT b.title, AVG(r.rating) AS average_rating
FROM books b
JOIN reviews r ON b.book_id = r.book_id
GROUP BY b.title
HAVING AVG(r.rating) >= 4;
```

Figure 6: Query the Data

5. Advanced Features

Leverage PostgreSQL's advanced features to enhance your literary data management:

Full-Text Search: PostgreSQL supports full-text search for searching large texts efficiently.

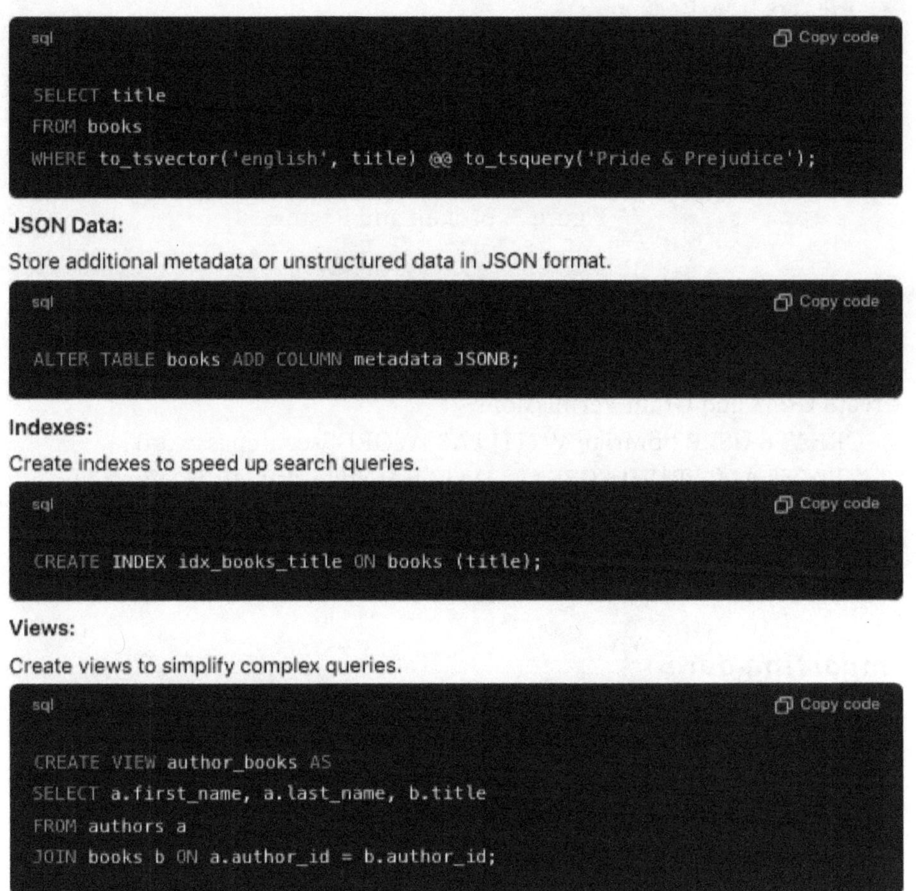

```sql
SELECT title
FROM books
WHERE to_tsvector('english', title) @@ to_tsquery('Pride & Prejudice');
```

JSON Data:

Store additional metadata or unstructured data in JSON format.

```sql
ALTER TABLE books ADD COLUMN metadata JSONB;
```

Indexes:

Create indexes to speed up search queries.

```sql
CREATE INDEX idx_books_title ON books (title);
```

Views:

Create views to simplify complex queries.

```sql
CREATE VIEW author_books AS
SELECT a.first_name, a.last_name, b.title
FROM authors a
JOIN books b ON a.author_id = b.author_id;
```

Figure 7: Enhancing your literary data management

6. Backup and Maintenance

Regularly back up your database to prevent data loss.

- **Create a Backup:**

```sh
pg_dump literary_db > literary_db_backup.sql
```

- **Restore from Backup:**

```sh
psql literary_db < literary_db_backup.sql
```

Figure 8: Backup and Restore

7. Security and Access Control

Create Users and Grant Permissions:

CREATE USER librarian WITH PASSWORD 'securepassword';

GRANT ALL PRIVILEGES ON DATABASE literary_db TO librarian;

PostgreSQL is a powerful tool for managing and developing literary data, enabling complex queries, data integrity, and detailed analysis through its powerful features.

Importing data

Importing data into PostgreSQL can be done in various ways depending on the format of the data and the tools you are using. Here's a guide to importing data into PostgreSQL from common sources such as CSV files, SQL dump files, and other formats.

1. Importing Data from CSV Files

Using COPY Command

The COPY command is a powerful way to import large amounts of data from a CSV file directly into a PostgreSQL table.

Steps:

Prepare Your CSV File:

Ensure your CSV file is properly formatted. For example:
title,publication_date,author_id,genre_id,isbn
Pride and Prejudice,1813-01-28,1,1,978-0141040349
The following steps are going to be followed by you:

1. **Prepare Your CSV File:**

   - Ensure your CSV file is properly formatted. For example:

   ```csv
   title,publication_date,author_id,genre_id,isbn
   Pride and Prejudice,1813-01-28,1,1,978-0141040349
   ```

2. **Create a Table:**

   - Create a table in PostgreSQL that matches the structure of your CSV file:

   ```sql
   CREATE TABLE books (
       book_id SERIAL PRIMARY KEY,
       title VARCHAR(255),
       publication_date DATE,
       author_id INT,
       genre_id INT,
       isbn VARCHAR(20) UNIQUE
   );
   ```

3. **Import Data Using `COPY`:**

   - Use the `COPY` command to import data:

   ```sql
   COPY books(title, publication_date, author_id, genre_id, isbn)
   FROM '/path/to/your/file.csv'
   DELIMITER ','
   CSV HEADER;
   ```

   - Replace `/path/to/your/file.csv` with the path to your CSV file.

   - `CSV HEADER` tells PostgreSQL to ignore the first line of the file as it contains column headers.

Figure 9: CSV Files

Note: The file path must be accessible from the PostgreSQL server. Alternatively, use \COPY in psql to avoid file path issues:

\COPY books(title, publication_date, author_id, genre_id, isbn) FROM '/path/to/your/file.csv' DELIMITER ',' CSV HEADER;

Using pgAdmin

Open pgAdmin:

Connect to your PostgreSQL server and navigate to the database.

Import Data:

Right-click on the table into which you want to import data.

Select "Import/Export Data."

Choose the "Import" tab.

Browse and select your CSV file.

Configure options like delimiter and encoding.

Click "OK" to start the import process.

Importing Data Using Python

You can also use Python libraries like pandas and sqlalchemy to import data programmatically.

Let's have an example:

1. **Install Required Libraries:**

```sh
pip install pandas sqlalchemy psycopg2
```

2. **Import Data Using Python:**

```python
import pandas as pd
from sqlalchemy import create_engine

# Create a database engine
engine = create_engine('postgresql://username:password@localhost:5432/yourdatak

# Load CSV data into DataFrame
df = pd.read_csv('/path/to/your/file.csv')

# Write DataFrame to PostgreSQL
df.to_sql('books', engine, if_exists='append', index=False)
```

Figure 10: Importing Data Using Python

PostgreSQL is a powerful tool for managing literary data, allowing for efficient querying and analysis. To import and manage data, ensure that the table's data types and constraints match those in the source. If errors occur during import, review the PostgreSQL logs and adjust the data or import commands as needed. Ensure that you have the necessary permissions to import data into the target database. PostgreSQL is widely used in scholarly works and projects, particularly for managing and analyzing literary corpora and text data in research.

Database Projects and Publications

Here are a few examples from scholarly projects and publications:

1. The Digital Thucydides Project

Project Description: The Digital Thucydides Project focuses on digitizing and analyzing the works of the ancient Greek historian Thucydides. The project uses PostgreSQL for storing and querying textual data from Thucydides' works.

Database Design: The project involves creating a schema to manage the text of Thucydides' history, including tables for different books, chapters, and sections.

Text Analysis: PostgreSQL is used to perform text searches and analyses, including word frequency analysis and text comparison.

Schema Example:

```sql
CREATE TABLE books (
    book_id SERIAL PRIMARY KEY,
    title VARCHAR(255),
    author VARCHAR(255),
    publication_date DATE
);

CREATE TABLE chapters (
    chapter_id SERIAL PRIMARY KEY,
    book_id INT REFERENCES books(book_id),
    chapter_number INT,
    chapter_title VARCHAR(255)
);

CREATE TABLE text (
    text_id SERIAL PRIMARY KEY,
    chapter_id INT REFERENCES chapters(chapter_id),
    paragraph_number INT,
    text_content TEXT
);
```

Figure 11: Create Table Books, Chapters, and Text

Data Import: The texts would be imported from digitized versions of Thucydides' works, which could be in formats like XML or CSV.

2. The Digital Library of the Caribbean (dLOC)

Project Description: The Digital Library of the Caribbean is a collaborative project that digitizes and provides access to Caribbean cultural and historical documents. PostgreSQL is used for managing the metadata and full-text content of the documents.

Database Design: PostgreSQL is used to create tables for document metadata (e.g., title, author, publication date) and full-text content.

Full-Text Search: PostgreSQL's full-text search capabilities are used to enable advanced search features for users to find relevant documents.

Schema Example

```sql
CREATE TABLE documents (
    doc_id SERIAL PRIMARY KEY,
    title VARCHAR(255),
    author VARCHAR(255),
    publication_date DATE,
    metadata JSONB
);

CREATE TABLE document_text (
    doc_id INT REFERENCES documents(doc_id),
    content TEXT
);
```

Figure 12: Create Table document Command

Data Import: Metadata and full-text content would be imported from digital scans and OCR results, often formatted in XML or JSON.

3. *The Literary Lab*

Project Description: The Literary Lab at Stanford University conducts research on literary texts using computational methods. PostgreSQL is used for storing and analyzing data related to literary genres, authors, and textual features.

Database Design: The lab uses PostgreSQL to store data on literary texts, including metadata and analysis results.

Data Analysis: PostgreSQL's analytical functions and extensions are used to perform statistical analysis on literary texts.

Schema Example:

```sql
CREATE TABLE texts (
    text_id SERIAL PRIMARY KEY,
    title VARCHAR(255),
    author VARCHAR(255),
    genre VARCHAR(100),
    publication_year INT
);

CREATE TABLE text_analysis (
    analysis_id SERIAL PRIMARY KEY,
    text_id INT REFERENCES texts(text_id),
    analysis_type VARCHAR(100),
    result JSONB
);
```

Figure 13: Create Table text command

Data Import: Textual data and analysis results are imported from various research sources, including digital archives and analysis scripts.

4. *The Perseus Digital Library*

Project Description: The Perseus Digital Library is a large digital library focusing on ancient texts. It uses PostgreSQL to manage a vast collection of Greek and Roman texts and their annotations.

Database Design: PostgreSQL is used to manage complex data relationships, including texts, translations, and annotations.

Textual Analysis: Advanced queries and text analyses are performed using PostgreSQL's features.

Schema Example

```sql
sql

CREATE TABLE texts (
    text_id SERIAL PRIMARY KEY,
    title VARCHAR(255),
    author VARCHAR(255),
    original_text TEXT
);

CREATE TABLE translations (
    translation_id SERIAL PRIMARY KEY,
    text_id INT REFERENCES texts(text_id),
    language VARCHAR(100),
    translated_text TEXT
);

CREATE TABLE annotations (
    annotation_id SERIAL PRIMARY KEY,
    text_id INT REFERENCES texts(text_id),
    annotation_text TEXT,
    annotation_position INT
);
```

Figure 14: Create Table annotations command

Data Import: Texts and annotations are imported from digital archives and scholarly translations, often using XML or JSON formats.

These examples illustrate how PostgreSQL can be effectively used in literary research and digital humanities projects. The database's advanced features, such as full-text search, JSON support, and analytical functions, make it a powerful tool for managing and analyzing literary data.

Conclusion and Recommendations

PostgreSQL is an open-source relational database management system that can be highly effective for literary research and digital humanities projects. It offers advanced data types, full-text search capabilities, and advanced querying features, allowing for flexible storage and querying of semi-structured data. PostgreSQL's built-in full-text search capabilities enable efficient searching and querying of large volumes of textual data. Advanced querying features, such as window functions, common table expressions (CTEs), and recursive queries, facilitate sophisticated data manipulation and analysis. PostgreSQL can be integrated with text analysis tools like NLTK, spaCy, or custom Python scripts, enhancing the ability to perform linguistic analyses, sentiment analysis, or thematic modelling on literary texts. A well-designed relational schema reflects the structure and relationships in literary datasets, ensuring data integrity, efficient querying, and ease of data management. PostgreSQL's PostGIS extension enables spatial queries and geospatial analysis, making it valuable for projects exploring geographical elements in literature. Data visualization tools like Tableau, D3.js, or Plotly can help interpret complex datasets and present findings in a comprehensible manner. Regular assessment and adaptation of the database schema and infrastructure to meet evolving research needs to ensure the continued relevance and effectiveness of PostgreSQL as a powerful and flexible tool in the digital humanities toolkit.

References

Blevins, C. J. The Perseus Digital Library: A Case Study of the Impact of Digital Libraries on Research. Digital Scholarship. 2009.

Coulson, H. "The Digital Thucydides Project: An Exploration of Digital Resources for Ancient Greek Texts." International Journal of Humanities and Arts Computing.2003.

EARHART, AMY E. "Data and the Fragmented Text: Tools, Visualization, and Datamining or Is Bigger Better?" Traces of the Old, Uses of the New: The Emergence of Digital Literary Studies, University of Michigan Press, 2015, pp. 90–116. JSTOR, https://doi.org/10.2307/j.ctv65swvf.8. Accessed 27 Aug. 2024.

Enslen, Joshua Alma. "The Word, the Database, and the Algorithm." Song of Exile: A Cultural History of Brazil's Most Popular Poem, 1846–2018, Purdue University Press, 2022, pp. 151–56. JSTOR, https://doi.org/10.2307/j.ctv1xg5h5p.12. Accessed 27 Aug. 2024.

Jockers, M. L., Macroanalysis: Digital Methods and Literary History. University of Illinois Press. 2013.

López, V. (2010). "The Digital Library of the Caribbean: A Case Study in Digital Library Development." Journal of Digital Information.2010.

Rahaman, V., Haider, A. (2021). Deconstructive Big Data Analytics: Literary Texts Analysis Through Atlas.ti Software. In: Sharma, S., Rahaman, V., Sinha, G.R. (eds) Big Data Analytics in Cognitive Social Media and Literary Texts. Springer, Singapore. https://doi.org/10.1007/978-981-16-4729-1_3

Rahaman, V., Agarwal, S. (2021). Necessity of Big Data Analytics in Social Media for Questioning the Existence and Survival of Women and the Marginalized People. In: Sharma, S., Rahaman, V., Sinha, G.R. (eds) Big Data Analytics in Cognitive Social Media and Literary Texts. Springer, Singapore. https://doi.org/10.1007/978-981-16-4729-1_7

RISAM, ROOPIKA. "Navigating the Global Digital Humanities: Insights from Black Feminism." Debates in the Digital Humanities 2016, edited by Matthew K. Gold and Lauren F. Klein, University of Minnesota Press, 2016, pp. 359–67. JSTOR, https://doi.org/10.5749/j.ctt1cn6thb.32. Accessed 27 Aug. 2024.

STALEY, DAVID. "On the 'Maker Turn' in the Humanities." Making Things and Drawing Boundaries: Experiments in the Digital Humanities, edited by Jentery Sayers, University of Minnesota Press, 2017, pp. 32–41. JSTOR, https://doi.org/10.5749/j.ctt1pwt6wq.5. Accessed 27 Aug. 2024.

Stones, Richard, Neil Matthew. *Beginning Databases With PostgreSQL - From Novice To Professional*. Apress, 2005.

Ullyot, Michael. "Augmented Criticism, Extensible Archives, and the Progress of Renaissance Studies." Renaissance and Reformation / Renaissance et Réforme, vol. 37, no. 4, 2014, pp. 179–93. JSTOR, http://www.jstor.org/stable/43446356. Accessed 27 Aug. 2024.

Website Resources

David Frick, *http://www.frick-cpa.com/ss7/default.htm.*

PostgreSQL, *http://www.postgreSQL.org.*

PostgreSQL and tools developed by Red Hat, *http://sources.redhat.com/rhdb/.*

## CHAPTER FOUR

Digital Creative Criticism

Digital Creative Criticism is a critical evaluation of digital media and creative content, focusing on how they effectively communicate ideas, engage audiences, and utilize digital tools and platforms. Key aspects of this criticism include analyzing content and form, evaluating interactivity and user experience, considering the cultural, social, or political context, assessing the originality and effectiveness of digital tools and techniques, and considering ethical and social considerations. The work often involves a combination of theoretical perspectives from fields such as media studies, art criticism, and digital culture, adapted to the unique characteristics of digital media. The evaluation of digital media involves evaluating narrative, themes, aesthetic qualities, design, usability, technical execution, and the use of emerging technologies like AR, VR, and AI.

Aspects of Digital Creative Criticism

Analysis of Content and Form: Examining the narrative, themes, and aesthetic qualities of the digital work, as well as its design, usability, and technical execution. Statistical methods have become increasingly influential in the literary arts, offering tools and techniques to analyze texts in ways that were previously difficult or impossible. These methods include text analysis and mining, such as frequency analysis, topic modelling, and quantitative literary studies. These methods help scholars and practitioners gain new insights into literature, explore patterns, and perform quantitative analyses. Topic modeling, such as Latent Dirichlet Allocation (LDA), Non-Negative Matrix Factorization (NMF), and clustering, helps identify abstract topics within a collection of texts. Quantitative literary studies use Lexical Diversity, Readability Analysis, and Complexity Metrics to evaluate the complexity of a text. Historical and Comparative Studies use Corpus

Linguistics to examine language and literary styles over time, while Machine Learning and NLP techniques classify texts into genres, sentiment classification, and text generation. Visualization techniques include Word Clouds, Network Graphs, and Temporal Analysis, which examine how certain themes or topics emerge and evolve within a text or across different works.

Interactivity and User Experience

Evaluating how interactive elements contribute to or detract from the overall experience, including the effectiveness of user interfaces, engagement strategies, and the emotional impact of interactive features. Humanities-inspired technology is an initiative to the responses of developed technology. It criticises anti-human and post-human agents in the developed technology.

Context and Impact

Digital Criticism is an interdisciplinary discipline that combines digital tools and approaches with conventional literary and artistic evaluation. It originated from the field of digital humanities, with a specific emphasis on the process of text encoding and the building of databases. The discipline uses computational methodologies, vast amounts of data, and sophisticated algorithms to scrutinize texts and artworks. The main focus areas of this field include the study of written texts, the use of computational and algorithmic methods for criticism, the development of tools for digital humanities, and the critique of digital art and media. Digital Criticism revolutionizes conventional critique by facilitating meticulous examination, unveiling novel interpretations, democratizing criticism, fostering collaborative endeavours, and questioning established concepts of creativity and authorship.

Technical and Creative Innovation

Assessing the originality and effectiveness of the digital tools and techniques used, including the use of emerging technologies such as augmented reality (AR), virtual reality (VR), and artificial intelligence (AI), digital criticism tries to control the bad impacts. Kathy Ann Mills' review essay, "A Review of the 'Digital Turn' in the New Literacy Studies, critically examines the impact of digital technologies on the field of New Literacy Studies (NLS). The digital turn involves rethinking traditional literacy concepts to include digital and multimedia forms of communication, challenging and expanding the definition of literacy beyond print-based skills. The integration of digital literacies into NLS requires scholars to consider how digital tools and platforms shape literacy practices and meanings. The concept of literacy has expanded to include diverse and multimodal practices, including understanding how people use digital media to create, share, and interpret texts in different formats. The digital turn has influenced research methodologies and pedagogical approaches within NLS, with researchers increasingly using digital tools and methods to study literacy practices. Mills also addresses challenges and criticisms related to the digital turn, such as the digital divide and the need for equitable access to digital resources. The review concludes by emphasizing the importance of adapting literacy studies to the digital age and suggesting future research directions.

Ethical and Social Considerations

Horace Freeland Judeson's essay "Rage to Know" (1980) talks about curiosity and passion as two important traits of scientists if they are used to lead science in the welfare of society. Digital criticism reflects on the ethical implications of the work, including issues related to privacy, representation, and accessibility.

Criticism of e-Literature

e-Literature, as a genre of literary works that employ digital technology, addresses critiques such as authenticity, accessibility, interaction, and preservation. It represents a dynamic and evolving field where technology and literature intersect, leading to innovative forms of storytelling and reading experiences. Digital ephemerality may restrict its worth and longevity, while accessibility and inclusion might be constrained. Interactivity may impact authorship and reader experience, and typical literary critique may not apply to e-literature. Cultural and ethical difficulties come from privacy and data security, and the digital world may intensify cultural appropriation. Preservation and archiving issues emerge owing to fast technical progress, and economic interests and monetization might impair the content and accessibility of e-literature.

Digital Criticism and e-Literature

e-Literature, or electronic literature, refers to literary works that are created and experienced through digital technologies. This form of literature leverages the unique capabilities of digital platforms, such as computers, the internet, and mobile devices, to explore new ways of writing and reading. e-Literature often incorporates multimedia elements, interactivity, and non-linear narratives, offering experiences that traditional print literature cannot.

Features of e-Literature

Digital Medium

Works are published and accessed via digital devices, including computers, tablets, smartphones, and e-readers.

Interactivity

Many e-literary works involve interactive elements where the reader's choices can affect the narrative or structure of the text.

Multimedia Integration

e-Literature can include text combined with images, audio, video, and animations to create a more immersive experience.

Non-Linearity

Unlike traditional linear narratives, e-literature may feature non-linear storytelling, allowing readers to explore multiple paths or outcomes.

Innovative Forms

It often explores new forms of writing and reading that are made possible by digital technology, such as hypertext fiction, digital poetry, and networked narratives.

Types of e-Literature

Hypertext Fiction

Stories that use hyperlinks to allow readers to choose their path through the narrative. Michael Joyce's "Afternoon, a Story" is the finest example. "Afternoon, a Story" is a groundbreaking work in electronic literature, first published in 1987 by Michael Joyce. It is a prime example of hypertext fiction, a genre that uses hypertext links to allow readers to navigate through a non-linear narrative. The narrative is composed of interconnected nodes, allowing readers to explore the story in various ways. The story also features an interactive experience, where readers can influence the story's direction and development. The story revolves around themes of memory, identity, and relationships, reflecting the complexity of human consciousness. The work was created using a hypertext system called "Storyspace," which allowed Joyce to experiment with narrative structures that were not possible with traditional print media. "Afternoon, a Story" is significant for its innovative use of digital technology, establishing the genre of hypertext fiction and influencing subsequent works in electronic literature. It remains a significant reference point in the study of digital narrative and interactive fiction. Overall, "Afternoon, a Story" demonstrates how digital media can be used to create new forms of literary expression, pushing the boundaries of storytelling.

Digital Poetry

Poetry that incorporates multimedia elements or interactive features. For instance, "Voyages" by Jason Nelson. Jason Nelson's "Voyages" is an innovative masterpiece in the realm of digital poetry, seamlessly integrating written words, visuals, and interactive elements to create a one-of-a-kind poetic encounter. The main characteristic of the work is the integration of multimedia, which enables readers to engage with the text in a non-linear way, thus improving the reading experience. Additionally, it provides a non-linear narrative structure, enabling readers to traverse through distinct areas and unveil several levels of significance. Use of visual and auditory components enhances the textual content and adds to the overall thematic resonance.

"Voyages" is notable for its pioneering structure, demonstrating how digital technology may expand the limits of conventional poetic genres. Furthermore, it showcases creative and experimental aspects of Nelson's work, pushing the boundaries of traditional ideas about poetry and storytelling. This work is a component of a wider trend in electronic writing that investigates novel and captivating literary structures using new technologies.

Interactive Fiction

The text-based Zork is the finest example of interactive fiction. Digital critics regard Zork as a groundbreaking text-based adventure game. It was first developed by MIT students in the late 1970s. It is considered one of the first and most significant text-based games, utilizing text to explain places, objects, and actions. The game features a massive subterranean environment with various sites to explore, where players solve puzzles, discover goods, and interact with the environment. The story evolves based on the player's investigation and problem-solving. Zork offers non-linear gameplay, allowing players to explore various places and solve puzzles in many ways. Its open-ended architecture allows multiple methods and conclusions, making each playtime unique. Despite being text-based, Zork provides a rich story experience, with its vivid and immersive setting and complex narrative.

Zork is a cornerstone of interactive fiction, illustrating how text-based storytelling and player interaction can generate interesting and immersive experiences. It established a precedent for how digital texts can be used to produce rich and interactive narratives. The game has had a lasting influence on the gaming and digital literary sectors, opening the path for future interactive fiction and inspiring the design of many text-based and graphical adventure games. The original Zork series has been followed by sequels and adaptations, and its impact can be seen in current interactive narrative and game design.

Generative Texts

Algorithms composed and programming poetic work "Taroko Gorge" is a masterpiece. Nick Montfort's "Taroko Gorge" (2009) is a digital poetry piece. The piece uses a generative approach, creating text dynamically by an algorithm, generating new variations each time it is viewed. The text is arranged visually to enhance the reading experience and contribute to the overall aesthetic. The piece is inspired by the Taroko Gorge, a scenic location in Taiwan, and uses programming to create the generative aspect of the poem. The non-linear structure of the poem allows readers to experience different paths and interpretations each time they interact with the work.

"Taroko Gorge" showcases how digital technology can push the boundaries of traditional poetry by incorporating generative techniques and interactive elements. It contributes to the ongoing exploration of how digital media can transform literary forms and engage readers in new ways. Montfort's interdisciplinary approach highlights interdisciplinary nature of digital literature, where coding and creative writing intersect to produce innovative artistic experiences. The work is an important example of digital poetry and interactive literature, demonstrating the potential of digital media to transform literary forms and engage readers in new ways.

Digital Criticism in Literature and Arts

Digital criticism of literature, often referred to as digital humanities, represents the intersection of literary studies with computational methods and digital tools. This field has evolved significantly over the past few decades, blending traditional literary analysis with new technologies. Here is a critical history of digital criticism in literature, highlighting key developments, debates, and impacts.

Scope

Digital criticism, also known as digital humanities criticism, uses digital tools and methods to analyze, interpret, and critique literature and the arts. It includes digital textual analysis, digital editions, digital archives, data visualization, digital narratives, interactive media, network and spatial analysis, computational creativity, critical theory, collaborative and community-based projects, educational and pedagogical applications, and cultural and historical contexts. Digital criticism offers new perspectives and insights into traditional and contemporary works, enabling scholars to create innovative scholarly resources and engage with literature and art in novel ways. It also offers a rich and diverse scope for exploring literature and the arts, fostering deeper understanding and engagement. See Figure 1.

Historical Background

Early Foundations and Beginnings (1950s - 1970s)

It was an early age of Computational Text Analysis. The use of computers in literary studies began with early efforts in textual analysis and corpus linguistics. Scholars like Friedrich Nietzsche and Jacques Derrida were among the first to engage with textual data in a structured manner, though not using digital tools. The 1950s and 1960s saw the rise of computational linguistics, where early researchers started using computers to analyze text patterns, although the field was still in its infancy.

Text Encoding Initiative (TEI)

The Text Encoding Initiative (TEI) is a widely adopted standard for encoding and representing digital textual data, crucial in digital humanities, historical research, and textual scholarship. It focuses on preserving scholarly and contextual significance, providing a framework for encoding various textual types, promoting data interoperability, and allowing for customization. TEI includes elements for hierarchical structure and specific textual features.

Formation: The Text Encoding Initiative, established in 1987, was crucial in formalizing the encoding of texts for digital analysis. It provided guidelines for encoding literary texts in a way that facilitated their digital processing and analysis.

Impact: TEI set standards for representing text in machine-readable form, influencing the development of digital texts and the methodologies for their analysis.

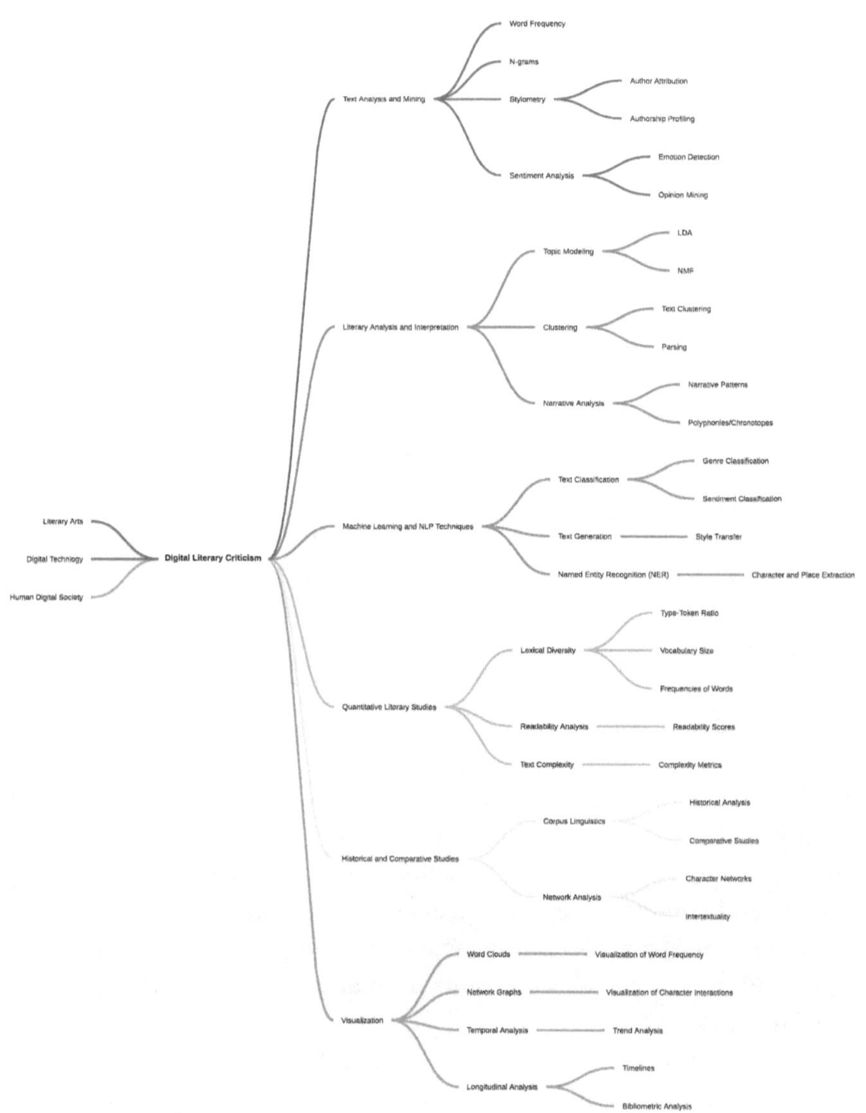

Figure 1: Scope of Digital Literary Criticism

Rise of Digital Humanities (1980s - 1990s)

Digital humanities is a multidisciplinary, integrative, eclectic, inclusive, and interdisciplinary discipline that blends conventional humanities studies with digital technologies and methodologies to promote research, teaching, and interaction with humanistic themes. Originating in the 1940s and 1950s, it has evolved quickly during the 2000s, incorporating numerous approaches such as textual analysis, digital editions, data visualization, geographic analysis, and network analysis. It was started with five major activities. They are:

- Textual Analysis: Utilizes computational methods to analyze large corpora of text, including text mining, topic modelling, and sentiment analysis.
- Digital Editions: Involves the creation of digital versions of historical texts and literary works, often with annotations, links, and interactive features.
- Data Visualization: Employs graphical representations to visualize patterns, trends, and relationships within textual and historical data.
- Geospatial Analysis: Uses Geographic Information Systems (GIS) to analyze and visualize spatial and geographic aspects of historical and literary data.
- Network Analysis: Analyzes relationships and interactions within data, such as social networks or character networks in literary texts

Emergence of Digital Humanities

Influential efforts include Project Gutenberg, the Internet Archive, and the Text Encoding Initiative. Digital humanities has altered academic curriculum, leading to new courses and programs focusing on digital technologies and digital research. Challenges include technical skills, money, and preservation. Future directions include breakthroughs in technology, better accessibility, and enhanced cooperation. The two early events are:

- Digital Text Projects: The 1980s and 1990s saw the rise of digital text projects such as Project Gutenberg, which aimed to digitize and archive literary works, making them accessible for textual analysis.

- Early Digital Criticism: Scholars like John Burrows began applying statistical methods to literary analysis, introducing computational techniques such as stylometry and authorship attribution.

Expansion of Digital Tools

Textual Analysis Tools: Tools like WordCruncher and TAMU's Voyant Tools emerged, allowing scholars to perform quantitative analysis on literary texts.

Critical Editions: Digital editions of literary texts became more common, offering enhanced functionalities like searchability and annotations.

Maturation and Diversification (2000s - 2010s)

Integration of Digital Methods

Text Mining and Data Visualization: The use of text mining techniques and data visualization tools became prominent, enabling scholars to analyze large corpora and visualize patterns in textual data.

Digital Archives and Databases: Projects like the Digital Public Library of America and Europeana provided extensive digital collections for research, allowing for more sophisticated analysis of literary and historical texts.

Digital Criticism and Literary Theory

Interdisciplinary Approaches: Scholars began to integrate digital criticism with traditional literary theory, exploring how digital methods could complement and enhance traditional interpretative approaches.

Critiques and Debates: There was a growing debate about the impact of digital tools on literary scholarship, with discussions about the potential for digital methods to overshadow traditional close reading and interpretative methods.

Impact of Social Media and Crowdsourcing

Public Engagement: Social media and crowdsourcing initiatives like Wikipedia and Zooniverse allowed broader public participation in literary and historical research, democratizing access to data and analysis.

Digital Editions and Annotations: Platforms like The Walt Whitman Archive and The William Blake Archive offered new ways to engage with literary texts through digital annotations and scholarly editions.

Current Trends and Future Directions (2010s - Present)

Advanced Computational Methods

Machine Learning and AI: The application of machine learning and artificial intelligence to literary analysis has opened new avenues for exploring textual patterns, thematic analysis, and even generating literary texts.

Network Analysis: Techniques such as network analysis are used to study relationships between characters, themes, and authors, providing new insights into literary structures and dynamics.

Digital Preservation and Accessibility

Preservation Projects: Efforts to preserve digital texts and ensure their long-term accessibility continue to grow, with initiatives aimed at safeguarding digital literature for future generations.

Open Access: The open access movement promotes the free availability of digital texts and research, fostering greater collaboration and dissemination of literary scholarship.

Critical Perspectives and Challenges

Ethical Considerations: The digital analysis of literature raises ethical questions about data privacy, digital rights, and the representation of marginalized voices.

Scholarly Impact: There are ongoing debates about the impact of digital methods on traditional scholarship, with some arguing that digital tools should complement rather than replace traditional literary analysis.

Digital Humanities in the Global Context

Global Perspectives: Digital humanities are increasingly incorporating diverse global perspectives, with projects focusing on non-Western literature and languages, reflecting a more inclusive approach to digital criticism.

The critical history of digital criticism in literature reflects a dynamic interplay between technology and literary scholarship. From early computational methods to advanced digital tools and interdisciplinary approaches, the field has evolved to incorporate a wide range of techniques and perspectives. As digital tools continue to advance, they offer new opportunities and challenges for literary analysis, reshaping how scholars engage with texts and contribute to the broader field of literary studies.

Forerunners of Early Computational Text Analysis

Early computational text analysis laid the groundwork for what has evolved into digital humanities and computational linguistics today. Several key scholars made foundational contributions to this field, pioneering methods and techniques that are still influential. Here are some notable figures in early computational text analysis:

Friedrich Nietzsche (1844-1900)

Though not a computational scholar in the modern sense, Nietzsche's work on textual criticism and his ideas about the philosophy of language laid the theoretical foundations for later computational approaches. His concepts about textual authenticity and interpretation influenced how texts were later analyzed using computational methods.

Ferdinand de Saussure (1857–1913)

He was a Swiss linguist, who played a crucial role in the development of linguistics and semiotics. His views, compiled in his *Course in General Linguistics*, set the groundwork for structuralism and semiotics. Saussure differentiated between *langue* and *parole*, concentrating on the abstract system of language. He established the notion of linguistic signs, which consist of signifier and signified, and maintained that the link between signifier and signified is arbitrary. His views have been critiqued for disregarding real language usage and the social environment in which language acts. Saussure's theories continue to affect numerous sectors in the humanities and social sciences.

Jacques Derrida (1930-2004)

Derrida's ideas on deconstruction and the nature of text have impacted digital textual analysis, though he was not a computational researcher. His theoretical framework inspired computational approaches to understanding textual meanings and structures.

Noam Chomsky

Noam Chomsky, a linguist, philosopher, cognitive scientist, and political activist is known for his theories on syntax and language acquisition. His work includes generative grammar, transformational grammar, Chomsky's hierarchy, universal grammar, poverty of the stimulus, and the minimalist program. Chomsky's theories have been criticized for underplaying social and cultural factors in language acquisition and focusing on syntax at the expense of semantics and pragmatics. Despite criticisms, Chomsky's work has had a profound impact on linguistics, cognitive science, psychology, and related fields. His work has also influenced language education and continues to contribute to linguistic theory. Chomsky's work has significantly influenced language education and continues to shape contemporary linguistic research and debate.

Roland Barthes

Roland Barthes, a French literary theorist and philosopher, revolutionized literary theory by contrasting the work as a fixed object and the text as a dynamic, interactive concept. He argued that the meaning of a text should be derived from the reader's interaction with it, not the author's background or intentions. Barthes also emphasized the role of the reader in creating meaning, arguing that meaning emerges through the reader's interpretation and the interplay of elements within the text. His ideas have influenced various disciplines, including poststructuralism, which questions fixed meanings and emphasizes the fluidity of textual interpretation.

John Burrows (1948-)

Burrows is a pivotal figure in Stylometry and computational text analysis. He developed techniques such as Burrows' Delta, which uses statistical measures to determine authorship and analyze stylistic differences between texts. His work in the 1980s and 1990s laid the groundwork for modern computational literary studies. His notable works include Computers and the Study of Literature (1987) and Delta: A Measure of Stylistic Difference and Its Use in Forensic Linguistics (2002).

Manning, Christopher D. and Schütze, Hinrich (Late 1990s)

Their book Foundations of Statistical Natural Language Processing (1999) provided a comprehensive introduction to statistical methods in natural language processing (NLP), which are foundational for computational text analysis. Although their focus was broader than just literary texts, their work influenced methodologies used in textual analysis. His notable work includes Foundations of Statistical Natural Language Processing (1999).

Mikhail Bakhtin (1895-1975)

Bakhtin's theories on dialogism and the heteroglossia of texts have influenced how computational methods are applied to analyze narrative voices and textual interactions. His ideas are often integrated into computational studies of literary discourse. Of many works, his The Dialogic Imagination (1981, posthumously) is a masterpiece and occupies a prominent level.

Alan Turing (1912-1954)

Turing's work in computer science and artificial intelligence laid the theoretical foundation for computational methods in text analysis. His ideas about algorithms and computation influence the design and development of tools used in text analysis today. His Computing Machinery and Intelligence (1950) is a well-known work.

Willard Van Orman Quine (1908-2000)

Quine's work on the philosophy of language and meaning has informed computational approaches to semantics and text analysis, particularly in understanding how textual meaning can be modeled and analyzed computationally His Word and Object (1960) is the best example.

James F. McDonald (1960s - 1980s)

McDonald's early work in computational text analysis focused on the development of algorithms for text retrieval and analysis. His research contributed to the foundation of modern text-mining techniques. Early papers on text retrieval and analysis methods (e.g., work presented in the 1970s and 1980s conferences).

Douglas Biber (1958-)

Biber's work in corpus linguistics, particularly his analysis of language variation and the use of statistical methods to study linguistic patterns, has influenced computational text analysis techniques. His Speech and Writing, (1988) and Dissemination are text-based literary data criticism of Western philosophy and Literature.

Susan Hockey (1949-)

Hockey's *Electronic Texts in the Humanities: Principles and Practice* (2000) is a popular reference in digital humanities. It argues that electronic texts have been foundational in understanding how digital tools and methods can be applied to literary studies and text analysis. is a contemporary DH work.

These scholars represent a range of contributions to computational text analysis, from theoretical foundations to practical methodologies. Their work spans different disciplines, including literary theory, computer science, and linguistics, and collectively has shaped the development of digital textual analysis as it is practised today.

John Burrows as a Textual Analyst

John Burrows is a prominent figure in the field of computational textual analysis, particularly known for his contributions to Stylometry the study of the characteristic styles of authors. His work has been influential in the development of methods for analyzing literary texts through quantitative approaches. Here's a detailed overview of Burrows' contributions and methods:

Background and Influence

John Burrows, a former Professor of English at the University of Newcastle, Australia, has made significant contributions to literary analysis by applying statistical methods to authorship attribution and stylistic analysis. His key areas of work include linguistic style study and computational text analysis. John Bradley has made significant contributions to digital textual analysis by developing XSLT tools and frameworks for processing and transforming XML-encoded texts. These tools are essential for encoding and preserving textual data in digital humanities projects, as they provide guidelines for encoding literary and historical texts in XML. Bradley has also contributed to TEI tools, which facilitate the creation, editing, and validation of TEI-encoded texts. Digital editions of texts, particularly those using XML and TEI standards, are critical for scholarly work, providing enhanced access to historical and literary texts. They include features such as textual commentary, annotations, and links to related resources. Bradley has also worked on tools for textual analysis, including software for statistical and computational analysis of text corpora. These tools help researchers perform various types of analysis, such as frequency counts, concordances, and comparative studies of textual features. Web-based platforms for texts have also been developed, providing researchers and the public with online access to digitized texts, allowing for interactive exploration and analysis. Examples of web interfaces for viewing and analyzing TEI-encoded texts include features for searching, browsing, and annotating. Collaborative projects involve the creation and analysis of digital texts, often involving multiple stakeholders and requiring robust tools for managing and analyzing shared textual resources. Bradley's work has significantly impacted the field of digital textual analysis by providing essential tools and frameworks for encoding, transforming, and analyzing texts in digital formats.

Burrows' Methodologies

1. Frequency Analysis

Burrows pioneered the use of frequency analysis of common words (function words) for stylometric analysis. These are words that carry grammatical meaning rather than substantive content (e.g., "the," "and," "of"). Function words are less subject to authorial manipulation and thus provide a more stable basis for distinguishing between different authors' writing styles.

Burrows' Frequency Analysis is a method to analyze and compare texts based on word usage, particularly function words (e.g., "the," "and," "of"). This technique helps identify stylistic patterns and distinguish between different authors or texts. It focuses on function words, which are less likely to be influenced by subject matter and more indicative of an author's writing style. The analysis involves collecting a corpus of texts, preprocessing, analyzing, constructing frequency profiles, and comparing these profiles to determine stylistic similarities and differences

2. Burrows' Delta

Burrows' Delta is a quantitative method to measure the stylistic distance between different texts based on their vocabulary and usage patterns. It helps in distinguishing between texts by comparing their vocabulary and usage patterns. The method focuses on the frequency of word usage, specifically the distribution of function words and other stylistic markers. The process involves text preparation, feature extraction, statistical measures, and distance calculation. The delta value is calculated by comparing the frequency distributions of function words in the text of interest with those in the reference texts. The delta value is then compared across different texts to determine their relative similarity or distinctness. Burrows' Delta can be used for authorship attribution, text classification, and historical and literary analysis. The exact formula involves calculating the chi-square statistic to quantify the distance between the observed and expected distributions of function words.

3. Principal Components Analysis (PCA)

Burrows' Principal Components Analysis (PCA) is a specialized application of Principal Components Analysis (PCA) used in stylometry and computational literary analysis. It focuses on function words and their frequencies, identifying patterns in word usage and stylistic differences between texts or authors. The method involves text preparation, normalization, feature extraction, and application of PCA. It helps in identifying authorship, classifying texts, and studying stylistic evolution. By reducing dimensionality and highlighting significant stylistic elements, PCA provides valuable insights into textual analysis and authorship studies.

Concept

PCA is a dimensionality reduction technique used to simplify complex datasets while retaining as much variability as possible.

Application

In textual analysis, PCA can be used to identify underlying patterns or themes by reducing the dimensionality of textual data (e.g., word frequencies).

3. His Works

Burrows' seminal works include Computers and the Study of Literature (1987), which highlights the potential of computational methods in literary studies, and Delta: A Measure of Stylistic Difference and Its Use in Forensic Linguistics (2002), which presents the Delta measure and its theoretical underpinnings for authorship attribution and stylistic analysis. These works laid the foundation for further development in computational stylistics and the application of statistical methods to literary analysis. Burrows' The Case for Computational Stylistics (2012) discusses the advantages and limitations of computational approaches to stylistics, reinforcing their role in understanding literary style and authorship.

4. Applications and Impact

1. Authorship Attribution

Burrows' methods have been employed in numerous studies to identify authorship of anonymous or disputed texts by analyzing stylistic features. For example, his techniques have been used to analyze works attributed to Shakespeare and other historical figures, providing insights into authorship debates.

2. Literary Analysis

Researchers use Burrows' methods to study stylistic differences between authors, genres, and historical periods, gaining insights into literary trends and influences.

3. Forensic Linguistics

Burrows' work has applications beyond literary studies, including forensic linguistics where stylistic analysis can aid in legal investigations.

5. Practical Considerations

1. Software and Tools

Tools: Various software tools and packages are available for implementing Burrows' methods, such as R packages for stylometric analysis.

Implementation: Researchers often use programming languages like Python or R to perform frequency analysis, PCA, and Delta calculations.

2. Data Preparation

Text Cleaning: Before analysis, texts must be preprocessed to remove noise and standardize formats (e.g., removing punctuation, and lowercasing text).

3. Interpretation

Contextualization: While statistical methods provide valuable insights, they should be interpreted in the context of literary and historical knowledge.

John Burrows' work in textual analysis, particularly his development of stylometric methods like Burrows' Delta, has significantly advanced the field of computational literary studies. His methodologies enable researchers to quantitatively analyze and compare literary texts, contributing to authorship attribution, literary analysis, and forensic linguistics. His contributions have laid a strong foundation for the integration of statistical methods into the study of literature, demonstrating the power of computational approaches in understanding literary style and authorship

Various Tools for Literary Databases

As demonstrated in previous chapters, MariaDB, MySQL, Python, PostgreSQL are usable software for literary criticism, conservation, and databases. In this chapter, we learn to develop literary databases. The chapter answers the question How can we start doing literary database projects through PostgreSQL?

PostgreSQL

Starting a literary data project with PostgreSQL involves several steps, from planning and designing your database schema to importing data and performing analysis. Can you start and manage a literary data project using PostgreSQL, leveraging its powerful features to handle complex data and perform in-depth analyses? Here's a structured approach to help you get started:

1. Define Your Project Goals

Determine the Scope

Define the type of literary data you want to work with (e.g., historical texts, modern literature, bibliographic information).

Establish the goals of your project, such as text analysis, bibliographic management, or full-text search capabilities.

Identify Key Data

Decide what specific data you need (e.g., book titles, authors, publication dates, text content).

Determine the format and sources of your data (e.g., CSV files, XML, digital archives).

2. Plan Your Database Schema

Design the Schema

Create an entity-relationship diagram to model the relationships between different types of data (e.g., books, authors, genres, reviews). Example Schema Design. Let's develop a book table

```sql
CREATE TABLE books (
    book_id SERIAL PRIMARY KEY,
    title VARCHAR(255),
    publication_date DATE,
    author_id INT REFERENCES authors(author_id),
    genre_id INT REFERENCES genres(genre_id),
    isbn VARCHAR(20) UNIQUE
);
```

Authors Table:

```sql
CREATE TABLE authors (
    author_id SERIAL PRIMARY KEY,
    first_name VARCHAR(100),
    last_name VARCHAR(100),
    birth_date DATE,
    nationality VARCHAR(100)
);
```

Genres Table:

```sql
CREATE TABLE genres (
    genre_id SERIAL PRIMARY KEY,
    genre_name VARCHAR(100) UNIQUE
);
```

Reviews Table:

```sql
CREATE TABLE reviews (
    review_id SERIAL PRIMARY KEY,
    book_id INT REFERENCES books(book_id),
    reviewer_name VARCHAR(100),
    review_text TEXT,
    rating INT CHECK (rating >= 1 AND rating <= 5),
    review_date DATE
);
```

Figure 2: Designing Scheme

3. Set Up Your PostgreSQL Environment

Install PostgreSQL

Follow the installation instructions for your operating system (Windows, macOS, or Linux).

Create a Database:
Connect to PostgreSQL using psql or a GUI tool like pgAdmin.
Create a new database for your project
CREATE DATABASE literary_db;
Connect to the Database:
Connect to your new database:
psql -d literary_db

4. Import Your Data

Prepare Data Files:
Format your data in a compatible format, such as CSV, JSON, or SQL dump files.

Use COPY Command for CSV Files:
Import CSV data into PostgreSQL tables
COPY books(title, publication_date, author_id, genre_id, isbn)
FROM '/path/to/your/file.csv'
DELIMITER ','
CSV HEADER;
Use psql for SQL Dump Files:
Import SQL dump files
psql -U yourusername -d literary_db -f /path/to/your/file.sq
Use Python for Programmatic Imports
Use Python libraries like pandas and sqlalchemy to import data programmatically:
import pandas as pd
from sqlalchemy import create_engine
engine   =
create_engine('postgresql://username:password@localhost:5432/

literary_db')
```
    df = pd.read_csv('/path/to/your/file.csv')
    df.to_sql('books', engine, if_exists='append', index=False
```

5. Perform Data Analysis

Query Data Using SQL:
```
    Perform basic queries to analyze your data
    SELECT title, COUNT(*) AS review_count
    FROM books
    JOIN reviews ON books.book_id = reviews.book_id
    GROUP BY title
    Use Full-Text Search
    Enable full-text search to query large text data efficiently:
    CREATE       INDEX      idx_books_title      ON       books       USING
gin(to_tsvector('english', title));
    SELECT title
    FROM books
    WHERE to_tsvector('english', title) @@ to_tsquery('Pride & Prejudice'
    Analyze Data
```
    Perform advanced statistical analyses or text processing, using PostgreSQL's analytical functions or extensions like pg_stat_statements

6. Implement Advanced Features

Create Views:
```
    Simplify complex queries by creating views:
    CREATE VIEW author_books AS
    SELECT a.first_name, a.last_name, b.title
    FROM authors a
    JOIN books b ON a.author_id = b.author_id
    Use JSONB for Unstructured Data:
    Store and query semi-structured data:
    ALTER TABLE books ADD COLUMN metadata JSONB;
    Create and Use Indexes:
    Optimize query performance by creating indexes:
    CREATE INDEX idx_books_title ON books(title)
```

7. Backup and Maintain Your Database

Create Backups:
    Use pg_dump to create backups:
    pg_dump literary_db > literary_db_backup.sql
    Restore from Backup:
    Use psql to restore data:
    psql -d literary_db < literary_db_backup.sql
    Monitor and Maintain:
    Regularly monitor database performance and optimize as needed.

8. Document Your Work

Document Your Schema:
    Maintain clear documentation of your database schema, data sources, and any specific queries or analyses.
    Share Results
    If applicable, share your findings with the community or your research audience, including any insights or contributions your project makes.
    By following these steps, you can effectively start and manage a literary data project using PostgreSQL, leveraging its powerful features to handle complex data and perform in-depth analyses.

Project Opportunities

Funding for projects involving literary data, particularly for Asian researchers, can be sought from various sources including government grants, international organizations, research foundations, and academic institutions. Here's a guide on potential funding sources and strategies:

1. Government Grants and Programs

National and Regional Funding Agencies:
    Asia Research Fund: Supports research across various disciplines, including humanities and digital humanities.
    National Endowment for the Humanities (NEH): Provides grants for research in the humanities, which can include digital and literary studies.

Ministry of Education, Culture, Sports, Science and Technology (MEXT) in Japan: Offers funding for research and development in education and culture.

National Research Foundation of Korea (NRF): Provides research grants in various fields, including humanities and social sciences.

Grants

Japan Society for the Promotion of Science (JSPS) Grants-in-Aid: For research in humanities and social sciences.

India's Department of Science and Technology (DST) Grants: Includes support for projects that involve technological applications in humanities.

2. International Organizations and Foundations

Global Funding Bodies

The Getty Foundation: Offers grants for research and conservation in the arts and humanities.

The Mellon Foundation: Provides funding for projects in the humanities, including digital humanities.

The British Council: Supports cultural and academic research projects with international collaborations.

Digital Humanities Specific Funds:

The Digging into Data Challenge: Provides funding for innovative research using large-scale data in the humanities.

Humanities Collaborative Grants by the National Archives: Supports projects that involve historical and literary data.

3. Academic and Research Institutions

University Grants and Fellowships

Many universities have internal grants and fellowships for research. Look into specific funding opportunities offered by institutions such as:

National University of Singapore (NUS)

University of Hong Kong (HKU)

Peking University

Institutional Research Centers:

Digital Humanities Centers: Many universities have digital humanities centres that offer grants or project funding.

Language and Cultural Studies Departments: Often have their grants or can guide researchers towards appropriate funding opportunities.

4. Non-Governmental Organizations (NGOs) and Professional Associations

Relevant NGOs and Associations:

Association for Asian Studies (AAS): Offers grants and fellowships for research in Asian studies.

International Federation for the Humanities (IFH): Provides funding for international research collaborations in the humanities.

Specialized Research Networks:

Asian Digital Library Network: Might offer funding or resources for digital humanities projects involving Asian texts.

5. Crowdfunding and Community Support

Platforms for Crowdfunding:

Kickstarter: Can be used to raise funds for specific literary and digital humanities projects.

GoFundMe: Allows for raising funds from individual supporters and communities.

Community and Alumni Support:

Engage with academic communities or alumni networks for potential funding and support.

6. Collaboration and Partnerships

International Collaborations:

Partner with international institutions or researchers to gain access to joint funding opportunities or grants.

Collaborative Research Grants: Many funding bodies offer grants for international research collaborations, which can be useful for large-scale projects involving Asian literature.

Let's take an example:

The European Union's Horizon Europe Program: Supports collaborative research projects across multiple countries, including those in Asia.

7. Proposal Writing and Grant Applications

Key Tips for Successful Applications

Develop a Clear Project Proposal: Outline your objectives, methodology, and the significance of your research.

Showcase the Impact: Demonstrate how your project will advance knowledge in the field of literary studies and benefit the academic community.

Include a Detailed Budget: Provide a clear and realistic budget for your project.

Highlight Collaborations: Mention any partnerships or collaborations with other institutions or researchers.

Resources for Proposal Writing

Many universities offer workshops or resources for grant writing. Seek advice from experienced researchers or grant writers.

For South Asian researchers

By exploring these funding sources and strategies, Asian researchers can secure financial support for literary data projects and contribute valuable insights to the field of digital humanities and literary studies. For South Asian researchers looking to fund literary data projects, there are several region-specific and international funding sources tailored to support research in the humanities, digital humanities, and related fields. Here's a list of potential funding sources and strategies specifically for South Asian researchers:

1. Regional and National Funding Agencies

India

Department of Science and Technology (DST): Offers grants for research, including those involving digital humanities and literary studies.

Indian Council of Social Science Research (ICSSR): Provides funding for research in social sciences and humanities, which can include literary projects.

University Grants Commission (UGC): Funds research projects and fellowships in various disciplines including humanities.

Sahapedia: Offers grants for projects related to cultural and historical research in South Asia.

Pakistan

Higher Education Commission (HEC): Provides funding for research projects in various disciplines, including humanities and digital research.

Pakistan Academy of Letters: Supports research and publications related to literature and cultural studies.

Bangladesh

Ministry of Education: Provides funding for research projects, including those in the humanities.

Bangladesh National Museum and the Asiatic Society of Bangladesh: May offer grants or support for cultural and historical research.

Sri Lanka

National Science Foundation (NSF): Provides grants for research in science and technology, including applications in the humanities.

University Grants Commission (UGC): Offers funding for research and development in academic fields.

2. South Asian Regional Grants and Foundations

South Asian Network for Professionalization of Parliament (SANPP):

Regional Grants: Sometimes provides support for collaborative research in South Asia.

South Asian Studies Council (SASC):

Grants and Fellowships: Offers support for research in South Asian studies, including literary and cultural research.

3. International Organizations and Foundations

Global Funding Bodies with Regional Interest

The Ford Foundation: Supports research and development projects in South Asia, including those in the humanities.

The Rockefeller Foundation: Provides funding for projects that address critical social issues, including cultural and educational research.

The Asia Foundation: Offers grants for projects that contribute to the development and understanding of South Asia's cultural heritage.

Digital Humanities-Specific Grants:

The Mellon Foundation: Provides funding for digital humanities projects, including those involving South Asian texts and data.

The Getty Foundation: Supports projects related to arts and humanities, which may include South Asian literary studies.

4. Academic and Research Institutions

South Asian Universities

Jawaharlal Nehru University (JNU), Delhi: Offers internal funding and research grants for projects in humanities and social sciences.

The University of Calcutta provides research grants and helps literary and cultural studies.

The University of Colombo offers internal grants for research in South Asian cultural studies.

International Collaboration Opportunities:

Collaborate with International Institutions: Partnering with institutions outside South Asia can open doors to joint funding opportunities. For example, working with universities in the United States, Europe, or Australia that have a focus on South Asian studies.

5. Crowdfunding and Community Support

Crowdfunding Platforms

Ketto: A popular crowdfunding platform in India that can be used to raise funds for research projects.

Milaap: Another platform for crowdfunding in South Asia, which can be used for academic and cultural projects.

Academic and Alumni Networks:

University Alumni Associations: Reach out to alumni networks for potential funding or support.

6. Proposal Writing and Grant Applications

Crafting Strong Proposals

Clear Objectives and Impact: Clearly define the goals and impact of your project, highlighting how it contributes to the field of literary studies and South Asian culture.

Detailed Budget and Timeline: Provide a realistic budget and timeline for your project.

Partnerships and Collaborations: Highlight collaborations/partnerships with other institutions or researchers to strengthen your proposal.

Proposal Resources

Workshops and Training: Attend grant writing workshops offered by universities or research institutions.

Seek Advice from Experienced Researchers: Consult with colleagues or mentors who have successfully secured funding.

South Asian researchers can access a variety of funding sources ranging from national and regional grants to international foundations. Leveraging these resources, crafting compelling proposals, and building strong partnerships can significantly enhance the chances of securing funding for literary data and digital humanities projects.

Completed DH Projects in India

There are several notable projects and research initiatives in India that have utilized PostgreSQL for various purposes, including managing and analyzing literary and historical data. Here are a few examples of how PostgreSQL has been employed in Indian research projects:

1. Indian Historical Texts and Manuscripts Projects

Project: Digital Library of India (DLI)

Overview: The Digital Library of India project aims to digitize and make accessible a vast collection of Indian manuscripts, books, and historical documents.

PostgreSQL Use: PostgreSQL is used to manage and query the metadata of digitized texts and facilitate full-text search functionalities. Researchers use PostgreSQL for organizing and indexing the textual data to ensure efficient retrieval and analysis.

Details on Implementation:

Schema Design: Metadata tables to store information about the manuscripts, such as title, author, and publication date.

Textual Analysis: Full-text search capabilities to allow users to search within the digitized texts.

2. Literary Analysis and Digital Humanities Projects

Project: Digital Corpus of Indian Literature

Overview: This project focuses on creating a digital corpus of Indian literary works in various languages, enabling researchers to perform computational analysis on literary texts.

PostgreSQL Use: PostgreSQL is employed to store the corpus of texts and metadata, as well as to support queries for literary analysis, such as word frequency analysis, sentiment analysis, and text comparison.

Details on Implementation:

Schema Design: Tables for storing text data, metadata about the texts (e.g., author, genre), and analysis results.

Data Import: Use of Python and SQL scripts to import and process text data from various formats (e.g., XML, JSON).

3. Archival and Cultural Heritage Projects

Project: National Mission for Manuscripts (NMM)

Overview: The National Mission for Manuscripts aims to catalog, digitize, and preserve manuscripts and ancient texts from across India.

PostgreSQL Use: PostgreSQL is used for managing the extensive catalog of manuscripts, including their metadata and digitized versions. The database supports the search and retrieval of manuscript information and facilitates research on these texts.

Details on Implementation:

Schema Design: Metadata tables for cataloguing manuscripts, including fields for manuscript titles, authors, and preservation status.

Full-Text Search: PostgreSQL's full-text search capabilities are used to enable searches within the digitized texts and descriptions.

4. Collaborative Research Projects

Project: Collaborative Digital Humanities Research Initiative

Overview: A collaborative initiative involving several Indian universities and research institutions to explore the use of digital tools in humanities research.

PostgreSQL Use: PostgreSQL is used as the backend database for storing and querying research data, including text corpora, historical records, and analysis results.

Details on Implementation:

Schema Design: Custom schemas to accommodate various types of research data, including text, metadata, and analysis results.

Data Integration: Integration of data from multiple sources into a unified PostgreSQL database for comprehensive analysis.

5. Data Management for Educational and Research Institutions

Project: University Digital Archives and Library Management

Many Indian universities use PostgreSQL for managing their digital archives and library systems, including literary collections and research documents.

PostgreSQL Use: PostgreSQL provides robust data management and search capabilities for handling large volumes of academic and literary data.

Details on Implementation:

Schema Design: Tables for managing books, journals, and other research materials, including fields for metadata and access control.

Search and Retrieval: Advanced search features using PostgreSQL's indexing and querying capabilities.

These examples illustrate how PostgreSQL is utilized in various projects across India to manage, analyze, and preserve literary and historical data. By leveraging PostgreSQL's powerful database features, researchers and institutions can handle large volumes of text data, perform advanced queries, and support digital humanities research. If you're interested in similar projects or looking to start your own, exploring these examples can provide valuable insights into effective implementations and use cases.

Wordsworth and TUSTEP

Wordsworth and TUSTEP are two different tools and methodologies related to the study and analysis of texts, particularly in the context of literary and textual research.

Wordsworth

Wordsworth is a software tool designed for textual analysis and the study of literary texts. It is useful in the field of literary studies and digital humanities. Here are some key features and aspects of Wordsworth:

Purpose

Wordsworth, the software, is used to analyze and compare texts in a structured way, often for literary research and stylistic analysis.

Features

Textual Analysis: It allows for detailed textual analysis, including stylistic and thematic comparisons.

Search and Retrieval: Facilitates advanced search capabilities to find specific terms, phrases, or patterns in texts.

Visualization: Offers tools for visualizing textual data, which can help in understanding patterns and relationships within the text.

Usage

Wordsworth is often used by scholars, researchers, and students to conduct in-depth analyses of literary works, compare different texts, and investigate various literary phenomena. A researcher, for example, studying the stylistic differences between two versions of a manuscript might use Wordsworth to compare word usage, sentence structure, and thematic elements systematically.

TUSTEP (Text-Und System-Tool-Entwicklung für Philologen)

TUSTEP is a comprehensive suite of tools for text processing and analysis developed for philologists and scholars in the humanities. It is designed to assist with the digitization, annotation, and analysis of textual data. Here are some key features and aspects of TUSTEP:

Purpose

TUSTEP is used for managing and analyzing texts in various languages and formats, with a focus on the needs of philologists and researchers in the humanities.

Features

Text Processing: Includes tools for digitizing, encoding, and formatting texts. It supports various text formats and standards.

Annotation

Allows for detailed annotation of texts, which is useful for adding scholarly notes, comments, and references.

Search and Retrieval

Provides advanced search capabilities for querying large text corpora and retrieving relevant information.

Statistical Analysis

Offers tools for statistical analysis of text data, such as frequency counts and pattern recognition.

Textual Criticism

Supports textual criticism by providing tools for comparing different versions of texts and analyzing textual variants.

Usage

TUSTEP is commonly used by philologists, textual scholars, and researchers working with historical or literary texts. It is particularly useful for projects that involve complex text processing and analysis. For example, a textual scholar working on an edition of an ancient manuscript might use TUSTEP to encode the text in XML, annotate it with scholarly notes, and perform statistical analyses to understand its textual history. Wordsworth is a tool designed for literary and textual analysis, focusing on comparing and analyzing texts in a structured manner. TUSTEP is a comprehensive suite of text processing tools tailored for philologists and scholars, providing capabilities for digitization, annotation, and detailed textual analysis. Both tools serve different purposes but are valuable in the field of textual and literary studies, offering unique functionalities to aid researchers in their work.

Digital Cultural Criticism and Database

Martha E. Williams' 1985 article "Electronic Databases" provides a comprehensive overview of electronic databases in scientific research and information management. The article highlights the technological advancements that have made electronic databases possible, such as computer technology, data storage, and retrieval systems. The benefits of electronic databases include speed and efficiency, data management, and remote access, enhancing collaboration and information sharing. They facilitate comprehensive literature reviews, support data analysis, and enhance the overall research process. However, challenges include data quality and accuracy, database maintenance, and user training. Williams speculates about future developments in electronic databases, including advanced search and retrieval features and new applications in scientific research. Ethical and security considerations include concerns about data privacy, intellectual property rights, and secure access controls. The article concludes that electronic databases hold the potential for further technological advancements and expanded applications in research. Alan Liu's essay "Where Is Cultural Criticism in the Digital Humanities?"

explores the intersection of cultural criticism and digital humanities (DH). He argues that DH often overlooks the critical and theoretical perspectives central to cultural criticism, which are underrepresented in the field. Liu advocates for a more integrative approach, where DH should incorporate cultural and critical theories to provide a more nuanced understanding of digital texts and technologies. He acknowledges the tensions between the technical focus of DH and the theoretical nature of cultural criticism and calls for a hybrid approach where DH scholars use digital tools while engaging with cultural criticism. He also calls for expanded methodologies to include cultural criticism, as it can enhance the field's ability to address complex questions about culture, technology, and society. Liu concludes by suggesting future directions in DH, advocating for a more inclusive approach that values cultural criticism alongside technical innovation. Douglas Eyman's essay "Defining and Locating Digital Rhetoric" explores the evolving field of digital rhetoric, highlighting its interdisciplinary nature and its adaptability to digital contexts. The essay traces the historical development of digital rhetoric, highlighting its emergence from traditional rhetorical studies and its adaptation to digital contexts. Eyman identifies core concepts and theoretical foundations of digital rhetoric, including the impact of digital technologies on rhetorical practices, the role of digital environments in shaping communication, and how digital media alters traditional rhetorical strategies. Key areas of focus include media ecology, digital composition, networked rhetoric, and interactivity and user agency. The essay also discusses the challenges and opportunities of defining and studying digital rhetoric, including the rapid pace of technological change and the need to adapt rhetorical theories to new digital contexts. It also discusses the practical implications of digital rhetoric for communication and rhetorical practice, noting how digital media influences message creation and audience engagement. Eyman concludes by suggesting future directions for the field, urging scholars to continue exploring the intersections of rhetoric and digital technology.

Digital Metacriticism: Digital Films on Criticism of Technology

Richard A. Lanham's "The Electronic Word: Literary Study and the Digital Revolution" (1993) explores the impact of digital technologies on literary studies and humanities. The shift from print to electronic media is altering reading and analysis, requiring new methods of textual analysis. Digital technologies challenge traditional forms of literary criticism, offering new possibilities for non-linear and interactive reading. Hypertext, a new literary form, creates a more interactive and fragmented reading experience. Digital publishing challenges traditional notions of authority and expertise in literary studies, impacting academic credibility and peer review. The book also discusses the cognitive effects of digital technologies, highlighting the need for digital literacy to effectively navigate and utilize digital resources. The potential for enhanced accessibility and democratization in literary studies is also highlighted.

In 2021, several documentaries explore the future of artificial intelligence, cybercrime, and the role of white hat hackers in protecting consumers. These include *Chakra, Cryptopia, Dark Web: Fighting Cybercrime, Dear Hacker, Drones, Hackers, and Mercenaries – The Future of War, MY.DOOM: Earth's Deadliest [Computer] Virus, Hacker Fairies, Hacker: Trust No One, Love Hard, The Perfect Weapon, Robot Apocalypse, Silk Road, The Mitchells vs The Machines, The Spy in Your Phone, Twenty Hacker, WANNACRY: Earth's Deadliest [Computer] Virus,* and *Black Warrant.* Each documentary highlights the importance of white hat hackers and their challenges in today's digital age. The rise of cyber conflict and the need for data protection are also discussed. The films help comprehensively understand the digital landscape and its challenges. The films explore the themes of cybersecurity and paranoia, with notable stars including Jesse Castro, Michael Einbinder-Schatz, and Leia Shilobod. Some of them are, namely, *Cyber Crime: The Dark Web Uncovered, Glass Onion, Glimpse, Hacker: Trust No One, Hot Seat, Keedam, Kimi, Pursuit, Stalked Within, The Takeover, @, Billion Dollar Heist, The Creator, Cyber Heist, Fast X, Heart of Stone, Invisible Hacker, Leave The World Behind, M3GAN, Missing, Reality Winner,* and *Unlocked.* These films demand the need for a comprehensive understanding of cybersecurity and its impact on the human race. They portray the result of unknowingness to the dangers of cybercrime, the origins of cybercrime, and the complex criminal organizations involved. The next chapter rests on these issues and discusses how these films have disseminated recorded impacts of growing technology over populations.

Acts of criticism of any such works require knowledge of database creation, design, and factors of leakages, and ways to control them. It is not easy to understand Science, STEM and Data fiction. Marie Lu's data fiction like the *Warcross series* requires a racial and gender discrimination sensitized person and a software engineering mindset gamer to understand their narratives.

Conclusion and Recommendations

Digital Creative Criticism is a concept that combines digital tools and methodologies with creative critical analysis to enhance and expand traditional forms of literary and cultural criticism. It emphasizes interdisciplinary approaches, promoting experimentation with digital tools, integrating theoretical frameworks, ensuring accessibility and usability, promoting open-source and collaborative projects, and incorporating data-driven insights. However, it faces criticisms such as overemphasis on technology, challenges of digital literacy, potential for obsolescence or data loss, and potential for exclusionary practices. Balancing innovation with tradition is crucial. By integrating these recommendations and addressing criticisms, digital creative criticism can contribute significantly to the evolving landscape of literary, art and cultural studies.

References

Anderson, Kate T., and Puay Hoe Chua. "Digital Storytelling as an Interactive Digital Media Context." Educational Technology, vol. 50, no. 5, 2010, pp. 32–36. JSTOR, http://www.jstor.org/stable/44429857. Accessed 27 Aug. 2024.

BODE, KATHERINE. "LITERARY STUDIES IN THE DIGITAL AGE." Reading by Numbers: Recalibrating the Literary Field, Anthem Press, 2012, pp. 7–26. JSTOR, http://www.jstor.org/stable/j.ctt1gxp79r.6. Accessed 27 Aug. 2024.

Das, S., & Ghosh, S. (2018). Digital Preservation and Access of Indian Manuscripts: A Case Study of the Digital Library of India. Digital Scholarship.

Clement, Tanya. "Multiliteracies in the Undergraduate Digital Humanities Curriculum: Skills, Principles, and Habits of Mind." Digital Humanities Pedagogy: Practices, Principles and Politics, edited by Brett D. Hirsch, 1st ed., vol. 3, Open Book Publishers, 2012, pp. 365–88. JSTOR, http://www.jstor.org/stable/j.ctt5vjtt3.20. Accessed 27 Aug. 2024.

Douglas, Korry. Postgresql. Addison-Wesley, 2020

Eyman, Douglas. "Defining and Locating Digital Rhetoric." Digital Rhetoric: Theory, Method, Practice, University of Michigan Press, 2015, pp. 12–60. JSTOR, https://doi.org/10.2307/j.ctv65swm2.5. Accessed 27 Aug. 2024.

Koehler, Adam. "Digitizing Craft: Creative Writing Studies and New Media: A Proposal." College English, vol. 75, no. 4, 2013, pp. 379–97. JSTOR, http://www.jstor.org/stable/24238180. Accessed 27 Aug. 2024.

Kumar, P., & Sharma, A. (2020). Building a Digital Corpus of Indian Literature: Tools and Techniques. Journal of Digital Humanities.

Lanham, Richard A. "The Electronic Word: Literary Study and the Digital Revolution." New Literary History, vol. 20, no. 2, 1989, pp. 265–90. JSTOR, https://doi.org/10.2307/469101. Accessed 28 Aug. 2024.

LIU, ALAN. "Where Is Cultural Criticism in the Digital Humanities?" Debates in the Digital Humanities, edited by Matthew K. Gold, NED-New edition, University of Minnesota Press, 2012, pp. 490–510. JSTOR, http://www.jstor.org/stable/10.5749/j.ctttv8hq.32. Accessed 27 Aug. 2024.

Mills, Kathy Ann. "A Review of the 'Digital Turn' in the New Literacy Studies." Review of Educational Research, vol. 80, no. 2, 2010, pp. 246–71. JSTOR, http://www.jstor.org/stable/40658463. Accessed 27 Aug. 2024.

Goodwin, Jack, and Eugene Garfield. "Citation Indexing-Its Theory and Application in Science, Technology, and Humanities." Technology and Culture, vol. 21, no. 4, Oct. 1980, p. 714, https://doi.org/10.2307/3104125. Accessed 2 July 2019

Nair, S., & Rao, M. (2018). Enhancing Library Management Systems with PostgreSQL: A Case Study. Journal of Library Science and Information Management.

RAMSAY, STEPHEN. "Humane Computation." Debates in the Digital Humanities 2016, edited by Matthew K. Gold and Lauren F. Klein, University of Minnesota Press, 2016, pp. 527–29. JSTOR, https://doi.org/10.5749/j.ctt1cn6thb.46. Accessed 27 Aug. 2024.

Rahaman, Valiur (2016) Introduction to Digital Humanities. Yking. Jaipur. India.

Rahaman, Valiur (2024) Teaching Digital Humanities in India. Notions.

Singh, R., & Bhardwaj, S. (2017). Archiving Cultural Heritage: The Role of Digital Libraries and Databases. Heritage Studies Journal.

Williams, Martha E. "Electronic Databases." Science, vol. 228, no. 4698, 1985, pp. 445–56. JSTOR, http://www.jstor.org/stable/1694720. Accessed

27 Aug. 2024.

## CHAPTER FIVE

Why Databases in Humanities Classrooms?: Teaching Next-gen Humanities Scholars

Generally, databases are not acceptable in the domain of humanities and social sciences. The question is why it should not be a part of teaching it to non-engineering background students. The database is a space of analysis and criticism and has become a space for several arguments, problems and solutions. We are nothing but bits in a database now. Our identity is recorded in a database. Our existence is measured through the database. It does not mean that humans have turned into android. Human is human android is android. They are irreplaceable. Mary P. Deming and Maria Valeri-Gold's article "Computers in the Classroom: Databases: A Hidden Treasure for Language-Arts Instruction" discusses the potential benefits of incorporating databases into language-arts instruction. It argues that databases are underutilized resources in language-arts instruction, but they can significantly enhance teaching and learning by providing students with access to a wealth of information and literary resources. Databases help students develop research skills, access diverse literary materials, support differentiated instruction, and promote critical thinking. The authors suggest incorporating database use into assignments, projects, and classroom activities to make the most of these resources. They stress the importance of professional development for teachers to effectively use databases in their instruction. However, challenges such as access issues, the need for appropriate technology, and proper training for students are acknowledged. The article advocates for greater use of databases in the classroom and emphasizes the need for teacher training and effective integration into educational practices. The authors conclude, "The uses of databases in the language-arts classroom can be as broad as the creativity of the students and teachers involved. Once students understand the basic concepts of databases, they easily move from a manual form to a more complicated and powerful computerized version."

In Patrik Svensson's book *Big Digital Humanities: Imagining a Meeting Place for the Humanities and the Digital* (2016), the main arguments revolve around the intersection of digital technologies and the humanities, exploring how these fields can collaborate and enrich each other. Patrik Svensson's concept of "Big Digital Humanities" aims to reimagine the humanities by integrating digital technologies into research. It emphasizes the need for interdisciplinary collaboration between the humanities and digital fields to address complex research questions and technological challenges. Digital technologies have transformed humanities research by enabling new methods of analysis, data visualization, and scholarly communication. However, Svensson also provides a critical perspective on their impact, highlighting potential pitfalls such as over-reliance on technology, the risk of losing traditional methodologies, and issues related to data privacy and digital preservation. He explores the role of the humanities in a digital world, emphasizing the importance of maintaining core values and methodologies while integrating digital approaches. It also envisions new forms of scholarly communication and dissemination, balancing technological innovation with traditional humanities research principles.

Why Databases in Humanities Classrooms?

Cybercrime sensitization

One of the biggest problems in human life today is cyber crime which starts with unethical hacking. The films highlight the importance of database knowledge, and related cybersecurity in today's digital age, with the threat of cybercriminals building machines that can attack public infrastructure. Films that represent technological dystopia and seed technophobia include *The Third Hacker, We Need to Talk About A.I., 21ˢᵗ Century Hackers, Chakra,*

Cryptopia: Bitcoin, Blockchains, The Future Of The Internet, Dark Web: Cicada 3301, Dark Web: Fighting Cybercrime, Dear Hacker, Drones, Hackers, and *Mercenaries – The Future of War, MY.DOOM: Earth's Deadliest Virus, Hacker Fairies, Hacker: Trust No One, Love Hard, The Perfect Weapon, Robot Apocalypse, Silk Road, The Mitchells vs The Machines, The Spy in Your Phone, Twenty Hacker, WANNACRY: Earth's Deadliest [Computer] Virus, Black Warrant, Cyber Crime: The Dark Web Uncovered,* and *Glass Onion.* These films explore the impacts and the future of artificial intelligence, cybercrime, and the role of white hat hackers in protecting consumers from digital threats. They also explore the challenges faced by white hat hackers, such as privacy issues, data storage, and government mass surveillance.

In 2022, several films were released, each with unique themes and plots. Some notable films include *Glimpse, Hacker: Trust No One, Hot Seat, Keedam, Kimi, Pursuit, Stalked Within, The Takeover, @, Billion Dollar Heist, The Creator, Cyber Heist, Fast X, Heart of Stone, Invisible Hacker, Leave The World Behind, M3GAN, Missing, Reality Winner,* and *Unlocked.*

Glimpse is a surveillance-footage thriller that follows three individuals as their lives spiral out of control. *Hacker: Trust No One* tells the story of a hacker who finds himself and his girlfriend on a hit list after getting mixed up in the shady world of cryptocurrency. *Hot Seat* follows IT expert Friar, who finds himself in the middle of a potentially explosive cyber robbery. *Keedam* follows Radhika Balan, a cybersecurity expert who falls victim to a cyberstalking incident and loses any semblance of privacy. *Kimi* is an action thriller that follows Gary, a home security operator, spying on a single mother using his company's technology equipment.

The Takeover is an ethical hacker who thwarts a cyberattack on a high-tech driverless bus, leading to her being framed for murder. The film titled @ is a techno-thriller starring Rachel David as an ethical hacker, focusing on the dark web and its horrors. *Billion Dollar Heist* is a documentary that explores the Bangladeshi Central Bank theft and the origins of cybercrime. These films provide a comprehensive exploration of the challenges and opportunities presented by the digital age, highlighting the importance of white hat hackers and the need for continued education and awareness about cybersecurity, database creation, safety and security. These films serve as a reminder of the ongoing threat posed by the digital age and the need for continued efforts to protect ourselves from cybercrime.

Interdisciplinary Collaboration

C.P. Snow's *The Two Cultures* concept posits a divide between the sciences and humanities, affecting intellectual discourse and societal progress. He argues that the scientific culture values empirical knowledge, while the humanities prioritize qualitative knowledge. Snow also highlights the lack of communication between these two cultures, which hinders collaboration and societal progress. He advocates for greater integration between the two cultures, promoting a more holistic understanding of complex issues. Although criticized for oversimplification, his ideas remain influential in discussions on interdisciplinary research and education structure.

A key argument is the need for interdisciplinary collaboration between the humanities and digital fields. Svensson emphasizes that successful digital humanities projects require expertise from both domains to address complex research questions and technological challenges effectively. Effective digital humanities work requires collaboration between digital experts and humanities scholars to address both technical and interpretative aspects of research.

Transformative Impact on Research

Patrik Svensson's *Big Digital Humanities* (2016) highlights the transformative impact of digital technologies on humanities research. Digital tools have introduced new methods, enhanced accessibility, facilitated collaboration, and challenged traditional practices. These technologies have increased access to scholarly resources, democratized access to information, and facilitated global networking. They have also led to new forms of scholarship, reevaluated methodologies, and encouraged interdisciplinary approaches. However, challenges such as data privacy, preservation, and the digital divide must be addressed. Svensson advocates for a forward-looking approach that balances innovation with traditional scholarly values.

Svensson discusses how digital technologies have transformed humanities research by enabling new methods of analysis, data visualization, and scholarly communication. He argues that digital tools and methods can enhance traditional humanities scholarship by providing new ways to explore and interpret data. Digital technologies have the potential to transform humanities research, offering new methods for analysis, visualization, and communication.

Critical Perspective on Digital Technologies

While acknowledging the benefits of digital tools, Svensson also provides a critical perspective on their impact. He discusses potential pitfalls, such as over-reliance on technology, the risk of losing traditional methodologies, and issues related to data privacy and digital preservation. A critical perspective on digital technologies is a comprehensive approach to evaluating digital technologies beyond their functionality and innovation, considering their impact on society, culture, and various fields of study. It helps scholars, policymakers, and users navigate the complexities of digital technologies, promoting equitable and thoughtful integration into society.

1. Influence on Society and Culture

a. Social Implications

A critical viewpoint examines the impact of digital technology on social structures, relationships, and behaviours. This encompasses the examination of matters such as the digital gap, privacy apprehensions, and the ramifications of extensive utilization of social media.

b. Cultural Effects

Critical perspective investigates the impact of digital technologies on cultural practices and values, specifically focusing on changes in communication, media consumption, and cultural output. This entails comprehending the reciprocal influence between technology and cultural environments.

2. Ethical and Moral Considerations

The critical analysis focuses on addressing issues around data privacy, surveillance, and the security of personal information. It raises concerns about how digital technologies manage user data and the possible dangers linked to data breaches. Algorithmic Bias refers to the examination of how algorithms and automated systems might potentially perpetuate or worsen prejudices and inequality. This can have varied effects on distinct groups and further strengthen existing societal biases.

3. Economic and Power Dynamics

a. Economic Implications

It examines how digital technologies influence economic institutions, including labour markets, corporate practices, and economic disparities. This involves investigating the implications of automation on employment and the power dynamics between tech businesses and consumers.

b. Power and Control

It analyzes who controls digital technologies and the power dynamics between technology producers, consumers, and institutions. This involves understanding how tech companies affect legislation, regulation, and public opinion.

4. Educational and Knowledge Implications

a. Changing Pedagogies

It looks at how digital technologies are altering educational processes and knowledge distribution. This entails analyzing the efficiency of digital technologies in education and their effects on learning processes.

b. Access and Equity

It considers problems of access to technology and the digital divide, emphasizing on how discrepancies in access might influence educational and professional opportunities.

5. Historical and Theoretical Context

a. Historical Analysis

It investigates the historical evolution of digital technologies and their antecedents, examining how prior inventions have affected modern digital environments.

b. Theoretical Frameworks

It applies numerous theoretical frameworks, such as critical theory, postmodernism, or socio-technical theory, to examine and explain the role and influence of digital technologies.

6. Future Implications

Speculative Analysis

It engages in speculative analysis of future technology advances and their prospective consequences on society. This entails anticipating future scenarios based on existing patterns and assessing their probable implications.

New ideas

It proposes new ideas and strategies to solve the issues and hazards found via critical analysis, intending to lead the responsible development and use of digital technology.

The Role of Humanities in a Digital World

He argues for the importance of maintaining the core values and methodologies of the humanities while integrating digital approaches. Svensson stresses that the humanities' emphasis on critical thinking, cultural context, and interpretation should continue to guide digital humanities practices.

Imagining New Forms of Scholarly Communication

Svensson explores how digital technologies can create new forms of scholarly communication and dissemination. He envisions a future where digital platforms facilitate broader access to research outputs, enhance collaboration among scholars, and engage diverse audiences.

Challenges and Opportunities

The book addresses various challenges in the digital humanities, including the need for digital literacy among humanities scholars, the integration of digital methods with traditional research practices, and the sustainability of digital projects. Svensson also highlights opportunities for innovation and growth within the field.

Big Data and the Humanities

Svensson discusses the implications of big data for humanities (Rahaman 2021) research, considering both the opportunities for large-scale data analysis and the ethical considerations involved. He argues for a balanced approach that leverages the strengths of big data while being mindful of its limitations.

Critical and Reflective Approach

A critical perspective on the impact of digital tools is necessary to ensure that traditional humanities values and methodologies are preserved.

Future of Scholarly Communication

Digital platforms offer new opportunities for scholarly communication and thoughtful integration with existing practices.

Balancing Technology and Tradition

Successful digital humanities projects balance technological innovation with the core principles of humanities research, maintaining a focus on critical analysis and cultural context.

Conclusion and Recommendations

Databases can be a valuable tool in the humanities and social sciences, aiding in research skills, personalized teaching, and critical thinking. Patrik Svensson's book Big Digital Humanities explores the intersection of digital technology and the humanities, highlighting the need for interdisciplinary cooperation to solve complex research problems and technical challenges. Digital technologies have altered humanities study by offering new ways of analysis, data visualization, and scholarly communication. However, Svensson also presents a critical view of their influence, stressing potential hazards such as over-reliance on technology, the risk of abandoning conventional approaches, and difficulties related to data privacy and digital preservation. The chapter emphasizes the importance of maintaining essential principles and techniques while embracing technology technologies. Successful digital humanities initiatives integrate technical innovation with the essential principles of humanities study, retaining an emphasis on critical analysis and cultural context.

References

Baum, Joan. "Science vs. Humanities: The Legacy of C. P. Snow." Change, vol. 13, no. 2, 1981, pp. 11–13. JSTOR, http://www.jstor.org/stable/40177438.

Borsheim, Carlin, et al. "Beyond Technology for Technology's Sake: Advancing Multiliteracies in the Twenty-First Century." The Clearing House, vol. 82, no. 2, 2008, pp. 87–90. JSTOR, http://www.jstor.org/stable/30194806. Accessed 30 Aug. 2024.

Clement, Tanya. "Multiliteracies in the Undergraduate Digital Humanities Curriculum: Skills, Principles, and Habits of Mind." Digital Humanities Pedagogy: Practices, Principles and Politics, edited by Brett D. Hirsch, 1st ed., vol. 3, Open Book Publishers, 2012, pp. 365–88. JSTOR, http://www.jstor.org/stable/j.ctt5vjtt3.20. Accessed 30 Aug. 2024.

Nguyen, Mong Thi T. "The Digital and Story in Digital Storytelling." Deep Stories: Practicing, Teaching, and Learning Anthropology with Digital Storytelling, edited by Mariela Nuñez-Janes et al., 1st ed., De Gruyter, 2017, pp. 72–89. JSTOR, http://www.jstor.org/stable/j.ctvbkjvdr.9. Accessed 30

Aug. 2024.

Pauwels, Anne. "Rethinking the Learning of Languages in the Context of Globalisation and Hyperlingualism." Plurilingualism and Multiliteracies: International Research on Identity Construction in Language Education, edited by Dagmar Abendroth-Timmer and Eva-Maria Hennig, Peter Lang AG, 2014, pp. 41–56. JSTOR, http://www.jstor.org/stable/j.ctv2t4b81.5. Accessed 30 Aug. 2024.

Rahaman, V., Haider, A. Deconstructive Big Data Analytics: Literary Texts Analysis Through Atlas.ti Software. In: Sharma, S., Rahaman, V., Sinha, G.R. (eds) Big Data Analytics in Cognitive Social Media and Literary Texts. Springer, Singapore. 2021. https://doi.org/10.1007/978-981-16-4729-1_3

Future Of Teaching Databases In Humanities

I quote my statements again in this chapter: "Generally, databases are not acceptable in the domain of humanities and social sciences. The question is why it should not be a part of teaching it to non-engineering background students. The database is a space of analysis and criticism and has become a space for several arguments, problems and solutions. We are nothing but bits in a database now. Our identity is recorded in a database. Our existence is measured through the database. It does not mean that humans have turned into android. Human is human android is android. They are irreplaceable."

Why teaching Database skills is connected to the future of teaching databases in the humanities. It holds both opportunities and challenges. They can enhance learning experiences by providing students with access to vast collections of primary sources, digital archives, and multimedia resources. Interdisciplinary approaches can encourage research by facilitating connections between humanities disciplines and fields like data science, computer science, and digital media. Digital databases enable collaboration among students, researchers, and institutions by providing shared platforms for data analysis and project management. However, successful collaboration depends on effective communication and coordination among participants.

The challenges include the digital divide and access issues, which may exacerbate existing inequalities, and the need for specialized skills training for both educators and students in digital literacy and data management. Preservation and sustainability concerns also need to be addressed, including data obsolescence and digital decay. Theoretical and pedagogical considerations include rethinking pedagogy, critical engagement with data, and ethical implications. By addressing these challenges, the humanities can benefit from the innovative possibilities offered by digital databases while maintaining rigorous and ethical scholarship.

Future of Teaching Databases in Humanities

Database teaching will be one of the popular pedagogical initiatives to make Humanities scholars engineers of society and human comprehension. Some major points are enumerated here:

1. Opportunities for Innovation and Enhancement

a. Enhanced Learning Experiences

Databases and digital tools can significantly enrich the learning experience in the humanities by providing students with access to vast collections of primary sources, digital archives, and multimedia resources. This increased access enables students to engage directly with historical texts, manuscripts, and other materials, fostering a deeper understanding of the subjects studied. However, the effectiveness of these tools depends on their integration into the curriculum and the pedagogical strategies employed.

b. Interdisciplinary Approaches

Teaching databases can encourage interdisciplinary research by facilitating connections between humanities disciplines and fields such as data science, computer science, and digital media. Interdisciplinary approaches can lead to innovative research methods and new ways of analyzing and interpreting data. However, this integration requires both students and instructors to acquire skills in both humanities and technical fields, which can be a significant barrier.

c. Increased Collaboration

Digital databases enable collaboration among students, researchers, and institutions by providing shared platforms for data analysis and project management. Collaborative projects can enhance learning and research outcomes by pooling expertise and resources. Nonetheless, successful collaboration depends on effective communication and coordination among participants, which can be challenging.

2. Challenges and Criticisms

a. Digital Divide and Access Issues

The effective use of databases in teaching depends on access to technology and digital resources, which may not be equally available to all students. The digital divide can exacerbate existing inequalities, with students from underprivileged backgrounds potentially having less access to necessary tools and resources. Addressing this issue requires institutional support and investment in technology infrastructure.

b. Skills and Training

Integrating databases into humanities education necessitates significant training for both educators and students in digital literacy and data management. The need for specialized skills can be a barrier to effective implementation. Institutions must provide adequate training and support to ensure that all participants can effectively use digital tools and databases.

c. Preservation and Sustainability

Digital databases and resources are subject to issues of preservation and long-term sustainability, including concerns about data obsolescence and digital decay. Ensuring the longevity of digital resources requires ongoing maintenance and investment in archival practices. Institutions need to develop strategies for preserving digital materials and making them accessible over time.

3. Theoretical and Pedagogical Considerations

a. Rethinking Pedagogy

The integration of databases into humanities teaching requires a reevaluation of traditional pedagogical approaches to incorporate digital methods and tools. This shift may challenge existing teaching practices and necessitate the development of new pedagogical strategies that effectively integrate digital resources into the curriculum. Teachers must balance traditional critical methods with new digital approaches.

b. Critical Engagement with Data

Teaching students to engage with digital databases critically involves understanding the limitations and biases inherent in digital tools and data. Students need to be trained in using databases and critically evaluating the data they provide. This includes understanding how digital tools shape research outcomes and acknowledging potential biases.

c. Ethical Implications

The use of databases in humanities research raises ethical questions about data privacy, copyright, and the representation of diverse voices. Educators must address these ethical concerns by teaching students about the responsible use of digital resources and the importance of ethical considerations in digital scholarship.

Conclusion

Hence, Databases in the humanities and social sciences offer opportunities and challenges. They provide access to vast collections of primary sources, digital archives, and multimedia resources, encouraging research and collaboration. However, challenges include the digital divide, access issues, preservation and sustainability concerns, and rethinking pedagogy. Addressing these issues is crucial for the future of teaching databases in the humanities, ensuring rigorous and ethical scholarship while addressing digital literacy and data management.

Can anyone say, "I am an expert in MySQL, though my area of study is Literature and Arts?" I visualize a time when equal weightage will be given to the Humanities scholars in recruitment drives of IBM, Microsoft, Apple, Google and the like giants in the universe of human technology. (Rahaman 2024) I visualize a time when no bird will be harmed, no data crime will occur, and no girl/woman/man will die of data leakage incidents. It will be a possible occurrence in the future history of "humanities-inspired technologies" (Rahaman 2019; 2020)

Reference

Rahaman, Valiur. "Perspective Chapter: Social Media through Digital Humanities – Why Not Educate the Non-Engineering Students?" In *Social Media and Modern Society*. Edited by Ján Višňovský. IntecOpen. London. 2024.

Rahaman, V., & Sharma, S. "Reading an extremist mind through literary language: Approaching cognitive literary hermeneutics to R.N. Tagore's play The Post Office for neuro-computational predictions." *Cognitive Informatics, Computer Modelling, and Cognitive Science*, 197-210. 2019. https://doi.org/ 10.1016/B978-0-12-819445-4.00010-2

Rahaman, Valiur, et al. "OBE Assessment Tools for Mapping Learning Outcomes Identifying Slow Learners: A Congruent Approach." Assessment Tools for Mapping Learning Outcomes With Learning Objectives, edited by G. R. Sinha, IGI Global, 2021, pp. 58-82. https://doi.org/10.4018/ 978-1-7998-4784-7.ch005

Rahaman, Valiur. Basic modeling of 'cognitive sensors' based on literary study of 'thick description' of human behavior. *Advances in Modern Sensors: Physics, design, simulation and applications*. 2020. https://doi.org/10.1088/ 978-0-7503-2707-7ch16.